ACTIVATING the PASSIVE CHURCH

lyle SCHALLER

ACTIVATING the PASSIVE CHURCH

DIAGNOSIS & TREATMENT

ABINGDON
Nashville

ACTIVATING THE PASSIVE CHURCH:
DIAGNOSIS AND TREATMENT

Copyright © 1981 by Abingdon

Library of Congress Cataloging in Publication Data

SCHALLER, LYLE E.
  Activating the passive church.
  Includes bibliographical references.
  1. Church renewal.   I.   Title.
BV600.2.S293   253   81-3460   AACR2

ISBN 0-687-00716-X

Scripture quotations are from the Revised Standard Version of the Bible,
copyrighted 1946, 1952, © 1971, 1973 by the Division of Christian Education of
the National Council of the Churches of Christ in the U.S.A., and are used by
permission.

MANUFACTURED BY THE PARTHENON PRESS AT
NASHVILLE, TENNESSEE, UNITED STATES OF AMERICA

To Samuel Emerick

CONTENTS

INTRODUCTION

Then the Lord God said, "It is not good that the man should be alone; I will make him a helper fit for him." So out of the ground the Lord God formed every beast of the field and every bird of the air, and brought them to the man to see what he would call them; and whatever the man called every living creature, that was its name."

Genesis 2:18-19 RSV

During the summer of 1976, while attending an American Legion convention in Philadelphia, an alarming number of men contracted a mysterious disease. Within a few weeks more than two dozen died. This lethal mystery disease was a front page story for several weeks. What was this deadly disease? What was the name of this illness that so often proved to be fatal? The newspapers and network news on television gave a big play to the story.

Eventually the Center of Disease Control in Atlanta gave it the name "The Legionnaires' Disease." Shortly thereafter the story disappeared from the front pages. Today people are still dying from this disease, but because it now has a name it is no longer a front page story. Today's stories about this disease do not even make the evening network news on television and usually are buried on page 26 of the *New York Times*.

All of us feel more comfortable if everything has a name. When a stranger comes to a meeting, everyone feels a compulsion to pause and take time for introductions. When a baby is presented for baptism, the minister asks, "By what name shall this child be called?" When a new school building is being constructed, the local board of education usually feels compelled to come up with a name for that new building before construction is completed.

This urge to "place a name on it" extends to types of churches. When a group of ministers come together, the introductions often include statements such as these: "I'm George Brown from Trinity Church, an inner city congregation in Cleveland." "My name is Ronald Johnson and I'm the pastor of an open country church ten miles west of Fremont." "My name is Henry Thompson and I'm the rector of a downtown parish in Portland." We all believe that if we can attach a descriptive label to our congregation this will help others understand a little more clearly who we are.

This intuitive desire to name things is behind one of the basic assumptions on which this book rests. It is assumed that if we can place a name on whatever it is we are dealing with, we will not only be more comfortable, we also will be more competent in handling it. A common example is the person with a pain who goes to see a physician. If the physician simply offered a prescription or recommended a treatment to relieve the discomfort, the patient would not be satisfied. The essential step in the entire process, for both the doctor and the patient, is that the diagnosis include a name for the cause or source of the patient's discomfort. This book represents an attempt to place a name on one of the most widespread sources of discomfort among Protestant churches.

Another basic assumption behind the writing of this book is that individual churches are different from one another.

INTRODUCTION

No two are alike. During the past two decades I have had the privilege of visiting over four thousand congregations from more than two dozen different denominational families. Each one has its own unique personality, its own distinctive mix of assets and liabilities and its own special place in God's plan for his kingdom.

A third basic assumption is that as our society becomes more complex, as the various denominational families become more pluralistic, and as new avenues for ministry and mission emerge, these differences among congregations become more pronounced. One result is that the differences, and the similarities, among congregations of the same general type, but from different denominational families, frequently become more significant in planning and program development than is the denominational affiliation. Therefore, each congregation must tailor its strategy for mission, adjust its priorities in the allocation of scarce resources, and plan its approach to program development to reflect and take into account these differences. These differences among congregations also influence the style of ministerial leadership that is appropriate for a particular congregation at a certain stage of its life. These differences have also made obsolete the old cliché, "Every minister should be able to serve any congregation."

The fourth introductory assumption is that, while individual congregations are different from one another, it is possible to devise a series of categories that enable one to group churches by similar characteristics.

The first chapter identifies a dozen different systems for classifying churches and also presents five major assumptions about the application of any classification to congregational life. This book is an elaboration of one of these systems, the idea of classifying churches according to their internal dynamics, rather than by the more widely used criteria such as denominational affiliation, or the geographical location of the meeting place, or the place of that congregation on a theological spectrum.

Interwoven into the analytical sections of the subsequent chapters are the insights gleaned from other useful, but often neglected, systems of classification such as the tenure of the members, the age of the institution, and the size of the congregation.

The second chapter consists of an effort to identify and describe the passive congregation. This is a diagnostic chapter intended to help the reader recognize the symptoms of this particular type of ecclesiastical pathology. One of the reasons for the extensive listing of the variety of the causes behind passivity is to enable the reader to identify more precisely the sources of passivity in a particular congregation. A second reason is the strongly held conviction that the prescription for passivity in any one congregation should be formulated in response to the specific causes or sources of the problem in that particular congregation. This chapter concludes with a thirty-question self-analysis exercise designed to measure the degree of passivity in your church.

In a majority of congregations afflicted with the complacency, lethargy, or passivity that is the subject of this book, the most effective response requires a redefinition of the role of that parish. This approach is based on the belief that the life and ministry of most churches can be conceptualized as a series of chapters. Frequently each chapter is written around a distinctive role or identity of that congregation. The new mission, for example, typically spends the first fifteen to twenty-five years of its life fulfilling that clearly defined role of being a new church. As the years pass, however, there comes an institutional maturity. It no longer is a new mission. By the twentieth year of its life, more or less, it becomes a mature church. At this point it either carves out a new role for itself, with a new set of goals to fulfill that new role, or it begins to drift. Periodically every congregation either redefines its role and identity or it tends

12

to drift into a passive state. The need to redefine role, the importance of defining role before formulating operational goals, and various ways of doing this constitute the third chapter of this book.

There are many other sources and forms of passivity in a congregation, however, and everyone should be equipped with a Plan B or a backup system. A dozen other sources of passivity, and the means to respond to each unique expression of that malady, are identified and described in the fourth chapter.

At this point some readers may be asking, "Why disturb the complacency of the members of that passive church? If they're comfortable and if their needs are being met, why get excited? Why not leave them alone? After all, weren't some of the major problems of the past twenty years created by excessively activist young ministers who came in and stirred up these complacent congregations? Why devote two long chapters to stirring things up? Why not leave well enough alone? Why not wait until the members are sufficiently discontented with the status quo to take the initiative in dealing with the passivity?"

These are fair questions and they deserve a response. This response can be divided into four parts. The first is that leaders do lead! This book is not directed at every member of every church on the continent. It is written for congregational leaders, both lay and ordained, who feel frustrated by the passivity of the church of which they are members. It is written to help these leaders diagnose the illness and to formulate a prescription to combat that passivity. It is written to assist the discontented leader, not to comfort the complacent member.

Second, the New Testament definition of a Christian fellowship does not support the contention that if the members are content that means the congregation is fulfilling its place in God's plan.

Frequently the complacent or passive congregation does

meet all the expressed wants of the members. Or, to be more exact, it frequently meets the social needs that are a product of that horizontal relationship of member and member. That, however is less than one-half of the two great commandments articulated by Jesus. The passive church is usually weak in its outreach beyond its own members and it is often weak in reinforcing the vertical relationship between God and the individual.

In other words, the passive church rarely meets both of the criteria laid down by our Lord in Mark 12:28-34.

Third, the limitations of the passive congregation are seen most clearly in its relationships to potential new members. Visitors come, they see the social needs of the members being fulfilled, but often the visitor leaves feeling his or her religious needs have not been met. One evidence of this is that in the average year the typical passive church receives a disproportionately small number of new adult members. More to the point, the passive church rarely is effective in fulfilling its responsibilities in evangelism, in offering a Christian witness in the community, or in social welfare and social action. The passive church usually offers less than is required in the area of an evangelistic outreach. The Great Commission (Matthew 28:19-20) rarely receives the endorsement it requires from the passive church.

Finally, there is the need for every congregation to be more sensitive to the distinctive needs of that new generation of adults born after World War II.[1] The research that has been done on this new generation of adults and on their outlook on religion suggests that the passive church will not be able to reach and serve many of these people, who view all institutions as inept. Whether one thinks in terms of institutional survival, or in terms of obedience to the Great Commission, it is a matter of great concern that the passive congregation appears doomed to be seen as irrelevant by at least one-half of all the persons born between 1945 and 1970. The passive church will not be able to help many members of this generation find meaning in life. That is certainly an important reason to be concerned about the role of the passive congregation.

There are many reasons why the churches should be concerned about their relationship with this new generation of young adults. After all, in 1985, 40 percent of the persons of voting age in the United States will be between 18 and 34 years of age. There also are many effective responses to passivity. Some, such as those described in the third and fourth chapters, can be planned and programmed. The three most effective cures of passivity, however, cannot be programmed that easily. One of these is a personal religious experience for each member. That is an event that happens within the life of the individual, however, and cannot be programmed on a congregation-wide basis. A second is the unexpected, and sometimes unsought, intervention of the Holy Spirit.

That, too, cannot be planned and scheduled by sinful human beings. The third is a flood of new members into the passive church. One of the first and most influential steps in encouraging that to happen is for the long-time members to view the newcomers as assets and not as liabilities. That is not as automatic as it may appear on the surface. New members tend to be different from long-time members in many respects. Several of the more significant differences and the implications for church renewal and for the pastor are the subject of the fifth chapter.

Some ministers are very content to serve a passive church. Most, however, are not. The greatest discomfort is probably found in the newly arrived minister who came with exciting hopes for the future and is greeted by passivity. There appears to be a somewhat greater chance of the new minister's encountering a passive congregation in those denominations in which the members turn to denominational officials for a recommendation for the appointment of a pastor, than in the denominations that expect each congregation to go out and recruit its own minister.

"We know every minister has a program. Tell us what your program is and what you want us to do and we'll do it," is a statement frequently heard by the newly arrived pastor of a passive church. Ten suggestions for a productive strategy by the newly arrived minister constitute the heart of the sixth chapter.

Every one of us carries around inside ourselves a complex assortment of assumptions about what constitutes contemporary reality. The first chapter analyzes some of the more widely held assumptions about the most helpful systems for classifying congregations. The last chapter raises questions about the assumptions of the reader. To be more precise, questions are raised about a half dozen of the more important assumptions that will influence a person's response to passivity in a church. Perhaps the most influential of these, in terms of a creative response to passivity, are the first and sixth.

This book, like every other book that is written today, is not the product of one person's thinking and experiences. Some of the published sources that may be of value to the more inquisitive reader are referred to in the notes at the end. In addition, however, I am greatly indebted to literally hundreds of pastors and thousands of lay persons I have met in parish consultations and in workshops, for their ideas, insights, criticisms, comments and reflections. In many cases I learned far more from them than they learned from me, and I am grateful!

Finally, this book is dedicated to a longtime friend, a former colleague, a generous and committed Christian, a wise leader, and a person who has remarkable gifts in creatively responding to passivity wherever he encounters it.

CHAPTER ONE

WHAT IS YOUR
CLASSIFICATION SYSTEM?

Back in 1880–1882, when the French were attempting to build a canal across Panama, they constructed several large hospitals. Patients were assigned to wards, not on the basis of the disease they had contracted, but by nationality. While this system of assigning patients to wards meant that everyone in a particular ward spoke the same language, it also meant that every ward had both yellow fever and malaria patients. One result was that three-quarters of the persons admitted to the hospitals died.[1] If patients had been assigned to wards by disease rather than nationality, the death rate could have been reduced sharply.

The Social Security system in the United States originated in the 1930s and classified the population into the two basic categories of workers and dependents. Forty years later that system of classification left the divorced wife, who often was neither a "worker" nor a dependent, outside the protection of the system.

The Southern Baptist Convention, which includes more congregations with a thousand or more members than any other Protestant denomination, offers two interesting sets of statistics. First, the 2500 largest congregations include approximately four million members. If they constituted their own separate denomination, they would be the fourth largest religious body on the North American continent. When that classification is used, the focus is on the four million members and on how these large congregations can reach more people.

At the other end of the size scale, the 23,500 smallest congregations in the Southern Baptist Convention also include approximately four million members. Any discussion of that fact of life usually results in focusing on that very large number of small and middle-sized congregations and on the needs and problems facing those churches.

These three examples illustrate one of the major assumptions on which this book is based. *The system of classification or the frame of reference used to describe a glimpse of reality influences the response to that subject.* The perspective often determines the response. If a person describes the tumbler as half empty, that evokes one type of response. If that same tumbler is described as half full, a different response is aroused. Likewise, the pastor who has been serving the same congregation for four years, and who views that as a long pastorate, will be far more likely to be open to a suggestion to move to a different congregation than will the minister in his or her fifth year of the current pastorate, who views the typical pastorate as lasting for at least seven to twelve years. The system of classification influences both the diagnosis and the prescription.

This basic assumption applies to every effort to help a congregation articulate its purpose, define its role, formulate goals and develop an action plan. The beginning point chosen for that process will influence the results of the effort.

There are many different approaches available for examining the life and ministry of a worshipping congregation, and no one approach will provide an adequate frame of reference for understanding all facets of church life. Each perspective adds something to help one see the total picture. The use of several different approaches in looking at a particular congregation will help one see the total picture more adequately, but each approach carries with it a distinctive bias. There is no neutral approach!

A parallel can be found in the study of American history. Traditionally the study of American history was undertaken from a political perspective with the chronology tied to political events. The economic interpretation, pioneered by Charles A. Beard, added another dimension. Frederick Jackson Turner introduced the frontier perspective. Merle Curti won a Pulitzer prize for his contribution to a social and intellectual interpretation of American history, as did Marcus Hansen for his examination of the impact of the migration across the Atlantic, and Andrew C. McLaughlin for his work in constitutional history. Each additional perspective helped students see the larger picture more clearly, but each approach carried a distinctive bias.

Another analogy can be found in the experience of the young couple who rented a vacation cottage for a week. One afternoon the husband looked out a window at the swimming pool and exclaimed, "Let's change our clothes and go get some exercise!" His wife, who was washing the dishes in the kitchen and looking out the window watching some people play tennis, quickly agreed. While she dressed for a tennis match, he put on his swimming trunks. The window a person chooses to look out at the world often determines that individual's perception of reality.

What Are the Alternatives?

There are many different windows available for looking at churches, and each one offers its own distinctive view. There also are many different systems available for classifying churches into a series of categories. Each one has its advantages and its limitations, and each one, when it is used, often produces predictable consequences. This fundamental assumption can be illustrated by reviewing a dozen of the classification systems used with churches. This brief review also will help establish the context for examining one type of congregation in greater detail and for reflecting on both the diagnosis and alternative prescriptions.

1. *Denominational.* The most widely used system for classifying churches on the North American continent today is the denominational affiliation. This is used in telephone directories, in choosing a seminary for the formal training of future ministers, in planning strategies for new church development, in scheduling and advertising lay training events, in planning the careers of the clergy, in the preparation of worship and teaching aids, and in scores of other ecclesiastical activities. Frequently, the application of this system of classifying churches produces a major emphasis on (a) institutional needs, (b) the needs and careers of the clergy, (c) real estate, (d) denominational programs, and/or (e) the importance of the individual's and the congregation's loyalty to denominational institutions, such as theological seminaries and missionary efforts.

From the perspective of the deonominational executive and of many pastors, this is often the most important system for classifying churches. Frequently, for example, these leaders will be acquainted with all the congregations of their own denominational family in their county, but have a very limited awareness of the ministry and programs of nearby congregations of other denominations.

By contrast, many lay persons classify congregations by whether they know persons who are members of that congregation, or by the pastor. "Oh, that is Reverend Peterson's church!" is the response when asked about Augustana Lutheran Church. "Sure, I know that church. That's where Jim and Helen are members, and they're our best friends."

This again illustrates the point that the professionals in the church tend to think in terms of functional categories, while the laity often conceptualize reality in terms of relationships. One result is that the professionals usually assume that when members transfer their membership from one church to a different congregation, these church members automatically will seek a church of the same denomination. While a great many lay persons do make a deliberate and conscious decision to find another church from that same denomination when moving to a new community, approximately one-half of all adult church members change denominations when they change congregations. They are influenced as much or more by the minister and/or the members as by the brand name.

If the focus is shifted from the orientation of the professionals in the churches and from the preferences of the laity, to the internal dynamics of congregational life, it seems the denominational label is of limited usefulness in understanding what is happening and why it is happening in a particular congregation. The size of the congregation, the median tenure of the membership, and the number of years that congregation has been in existence are three equally objective systems for classifying churches. Each one is at least equally useful in understanding the dynamics of congregational life. In other words, do not give too much weight to the use of the denominational brand name in classifying churches! Try a few other systems for classifying churches.

2. *Theological.* This system also is often used by scholars and other professionals as well as by many of the laity in defining the distinctive nature of a particular worshiping congregation. The use of this approach may direct the discussion to such subjects as (a) the importance of the various sacraments, ordinances and other religious rituals, (b) the differences among congregations with the same denominational heritage, (c) the role of the laity, or (d) the differences between the theologically liberal congregations and those that are conservative or in the middle of the theological road.

This system of classifying churches is frequently com-

21

bined with the use of the denominational affiliation to describe a particular congregation. "That is a very conservative United Presbyterian church." "That's a liberal Methodist congregation." "That's the only charismatic Lutheran parish in this county." "That's really an Anglo-Catholic Episcopalian parish." "That is the second most conservative church in the whole Southern Baptist Convention!" These comments illustrate the everyday use of this approach to classifying churches.

The use of theological categories also is useful in understanding which avenues of specialized ministries may be open and which may be closed. A simple illustration is a ministry with currently divorced persons. For example, the 500-member congregation with a cross section of the American population, age 13 and over, in the membership would include ten or eleven currently divorced men and sixteen or seventeen currently divorced women. Most congregations, however, convey the impression that non-members who are divorced are unwelcome. In response to this unmet need, several theologically liberal United Church of Christ congregations have developed a specialized ministry with divorced persons. In one of these, 32 percent of today's adult members are currently divorced. By contrast, many theologically conservative congregations have closed the door to most divorced persons.

The theological stance of a congregation is a useful frame of reference for understanding why permission is granted in some areas of ministry and why permission may be withheld for other proposed ministries. Likewise, the theological stance of a congregation is often a very influential factor in shaping the members' expectations of the pastor. The typical average workday of the pastor of a theologically conservative congregation probably will bear only a limited resemblance to the workday of the minister serving a very liberal church.

3. *Biblical.* This perspective frequently is used by leaders seeking a beginning point for defining the purpose of a

congregation, for identifying the role of the laity, for understanding the obligations and responsibilities of the ordained minister, for setting priorities among scarce resources, for developing a system of church government, and for formulating titles for the various offices held by church leaders.[2]

Perhaps the most common use of this system for classifying churches is in denominational political contests. The surface struggle usually appears to be over conflicting approaches to interpreting the Bible. The debate may be in broad terms over the question of the inerrancy of the Scriptures, or it may be focused more sharply on a single issue, such as the role of women in the church, the showing of motion pictures in a church building, the drinking of alcoholic beverages by church members, the use of instrumental music, the requirements of persons being presented for baptism, the power of bishops, human sexuality, the amount of formal education required of the ordained ministry, or participation in interchurch cooperation.

Sometimes these debates over interpretation of the Bible turn into struggles for political power and produce a series of categories for classifying churches such as "liberal," "conservative," "moderate," "cooperative," "loyal," "believers," and "non-believers."

In general, the more theologically conservative a person's perspective, the more likely it is that that person will use a biblical frame of reference, both for classifying churches and for evaluating candidates for ecclesiastical office.

4. *Community Context.* This system of classification was widely used during the last half of the nineteenth century and the first several decades of the twentieth century to identify the differences among congregations on the basis of the community setting.[3] The most widely used example was the simple two-category classification of rural or urban. Other examples of categories based on the community context

system include "the suburban church," "the village church," "Old First Church downtown," "the open country church" and "the church in the racially changing neighborhood." The application of this system often directs the subsequent discussion toward such subjects as (a) the discovery that this congregation serves only a small proportion of the residents who live near the meeting place, (b) the appropriate location for the building housing that congregation, (c) the need for renovating or remodeling the building, (d) the primary focal point in planning the new member recruitment system for that congregation, and/or (e) the mobility of the population.

In recent decades it has become increasingly apparent to many professionals in the churches that this system of classification has severe limitations. It once was believed by many denominational leaders that the community context was *the* critical variable in understanding the internal dynamics of a congregation and in its planning for ministry. Gradually, however, it has become apparent that, with the exception of the first residents of new housing, people do not socialize primarily on the basis of geographical proximity. People tend to socialize with other people on the basis of kinship ties, occupation or profession or vocation, membership in voluntary associations, and within social class categories, not on the basis of place of residence. The place of residence is no longer as closely related to the place of work as it once was. Neither is the place of residence as closely related to the place for retail shopping, recreation, dining out, or worship as it once was.

In other words, with the possible exception of new congregations started out in areas where there is a large quantity of new housing occupied by the first residents, very few religious congregations function as geographical parishes. This is especially true of (a) Black churches, (b) theologically conservative congregations, (c) urban churches, (d) long-established churches, regardless of

24

denominational affiliation or place on the theological spectrum, (e) a large proportion of all Roman Catholic congregations in the United States, (f) congregations with an aggressive and effective new member recruitment program, and (g) churches with a distinctive nationality or language identity such as Korean, Mexican-American, German, Portuguese, Haitian, Chinese, Filipino, Cuban, or Columbian. The big exception to that generalization is the geographical parish church in some rural communities.

As the world has changed from being primarily a rural culture to an urban society, the use of the community context has become less useful as a system for classifying congregations in order to understand their inner workings. This is especially true in such places as Akron, Ann Arbor, Atlanta, Boston, Buffalo, Denver, El Paso, Fort Wayne, Honolulu, Houston, Los Angeles, Memphis, Miami, Montreal, Orlando, Salt Lake City, San Antonio, San Francisco, Toronto, Tucson, Wichita, Winnipeg, and hundreds of other urbanized communities.

5. *Size.* From a pragmatic perspective, one of the most useful systems for classifying churches is by the size of the membership, or better yet, by size in terms of average attendance at worship.[4] This is not a new insight! Writing in the early 1930s, two eminent sociologists, each of whom had specialized for many years in classifying churches in terms of the community context, observed "The real difference is not between the church in the small city and in the large, but between churches of different sizes; for larger churches everywhere strongly tend to have more complicated organization, to employ staffs of paid workers, instead of the single pastor and to undertake varied programs."[5] A quarter of a century later a distinguished student of the rural church declared, "It appears that it would be more advantageous to study (churches) in terms of size . . . than in terms of location."[6]

Size, whether measured in terms of membership, worship

attendance, or Sunday school attendance, is probably the simplest single classification scheme for identifying the distinctive characteristics of a congregation. Frequently it is far more meaningful than denominational affiliation or community context as a means of understanding the differences among churches.

The use of size as the basic system for classifying churches into subgroups tends to direct the subsequent discussion to such topics as (a) the differences in organizational complexity, (b) the role of the laity, (c) the members' expectations of the pastor and the role of other paid staff members, (d) the potential for numerical growth, (e) the priorities in program development, (f) the appropriate size for a viable congregation, (g) the special needs of the smaller churches, and (h) the obligation of the very large congregations to share their resources.

Three examples can be cited to illustrate the value of using numerical size as a useful system for classifying churches. First, as the size of the congregation increases, the members tend to become increasingly dependent on the pastor to function as an initiating leader. The decision-making processes in the small congregation tend to be dominated by the laity, while in the very large churches the pastor usually is the most influential figure in setting direction and formulating priorities.

Second, the larger the congregation, the greater the importance of music in the life of that church. Small churches can function very effectively without a systematic music program, and many do not have a choir. As size goes up, however, there is a greater demand for a comprehensive and carefully planned music program.[7]

Third, the larger the congregation, the greater the probability that a long vacancy period between pastorates will produce a numerical decline in participation. By contrast, many small congregations thrive during the vacancy period. That long vacancy period provides "lay run" organizations more opportunities for the laity to practice their gifts and skills.

6. *Age*. While it is rarely used, except on an informal basis, there is a growing body of evidence that suggests that the chronological age of a congregation as an institution (this is largely unrelated to the age of the members) can be a useful yardstick for classifying congregations into various meaningful categories. For example, relatively new congregations are more likely to reach and attract the unchurched than are long-established congregations. Likewise new congregations often are more receptive to encouraging new members to fill important policy-making positions than are long-established churches.

In general, the longer a congregation has been in existence, the more vulnerable it is to the Second Law of Thermodynamics. This basic principle of physics, which has been applied to the life of organizations during the past half century, declares that every functioning organization produces predictable degrees of entropy. The energy put into an organization is never fully utilized for productive purposes. Eventually everything runs down as useless entropy increases. One application of this concept is that the recently arrived pastor usually exerts a greater impact on the twelve-year-old congregation than would be felt by the arrival of that same minister as the new pastor of an eighty-five-year-old church. The longer the congregation has been in existence, the greater is the amount of energy required to alter the status quo.

In general terms, the longer a congregation has been in existence *and meeting in the same building,* the greater the difficulty it encounters in reaching unchurched persons, the stronger the loyalty of the members, the greater the opposition to innovation, the longer the delay in accepting new members into policy-making positions of leadership, the stronger the orientation toward the members, the greater the attachment to that sacred place, the heavier the weight of tradition, the less oriented it is to persons who live in the vicinity of the meeting place and the greater the chances that the median age of the membership will be older than the median age of the residents of that community. (Some long-established congregations meeting in a building in the open country constitute the major exception to this set of generalizations.)

7. *Tenure.* While it is rarely used, one of the most revealing systems for understanding why all congregations do not behave in the same way is to look at the tenure of today's members. What proportion of the adult (age 18 and over) members have been members of this congregation for forty or more years? For thirty-one to forty years? For twenty-one to thirty years? For eleven to twenty years? For ten years or less?

While there are many exceptions to this generalization, there is a tendency in those congregations, in which most of the members have been in that same congregation for fifteen years or longer, for the members' loyalty to that congregation to greatly exceed the loyalty to the pastor. This is the opposite of what is usually true in the ten- to fifteen-year-old congregation still served by the original pastor. When that pastor leaves, it is easy for many of the members to drop out or to move to another church. In those congregations, however, in which the median tenure of today's members is fifteen years or longer, a change of pastors usually produces very few ripples, and these often are confined to the minority of recent new members.

Other generalizations that can be related to the tenure of members are, the longer the median tenure (a) the more difficult it is for a recently arrived minister to win the allegiance of the members, (b) the easier it is to launch a movement to seek the pastor's resignation, (c) the higher the level of financial support by the members, *especially in emergencies,* (d) the greater the probability that the membership roster includes the names of several alienated

28

and angry older ex-leaders who are dissatisfied with today's state of affairs, (e) the stronger the resistance to change, (f) the less likely that congregation will be able to reach, attract and assimilate new members, (g) the stronger the attachment to that meeting place and the more likely the congregation will display several of the characteristics of passivity described later in this volume.

Classifying churches according to the tenure of the members promises to be one of the most useful approaches to identifying and explaining the differences among congregations.

8. *Age of the Members.* One of the standard questions asked in most congregational self-study guides is directed at the distribution of the membership by age and gender. The preparation of the standard "age-sex pyramid" is usually offered as an objective demographic tool. The name and design of the usual graph carries with it a bias, however, that suggests the ideal congregation will include a large number of children, a decreasing proportion of older members and a fifty-fifty balance between males and females.

This device is an outstanding illustration of how the system of classification influences subsequent decisions. In the majority of churches today, preparation of the standard age-sex pyramid will cause the leaders to conclude (a) we have too many older persons and too few children and youth of elementary and high school age, (b) we have an excess of females and a shortage of males, and (c) if we don't make a ministry to young families our top priority, we will be out of business in another decade or two. The most useful general response to that entire process is "Nonsense!"

A better response would be to declare, "That is a natural and predictable pattern considering the aging of the population, the 'birth dearth' of the late 1960s and 1970s, the fact that this is a long-established congregation, and the strong loyalty of our members to our congregation. Now, how can we use these data to strengthen, reinforce and expand our ministry?"

While looking at the age of the members is a widely used approach (especially by congregational leaders) for classifying churches, it has several serious limitations. One of these is the temptation to use the life cycle of the individual as a model for the worshiping congregation. This may lead people to conclude that the eighty-year-old congregation, like the eighty-year-old person, has a very limited future. A second limitation was identified earlier; an excessive emphasis on the age of the members may tempt the leaders to seek to concentrate on reaching young families rather than on identifying, affirming, and building on strengths and resources.

In general terms, the younger the members, *and especially the leaders*, the stronger the future-orientation, the greater the willingness to take risks and the higher the turnover rate within the membership. The older the members, the greater the probability there will be a great interest in recreating yesterday, the stronger the loyalty of the members to the denomination and the larger the number of one-member households.

9. *Polity*. While it is not widely used, the polity, or system of congregational self-government, can be a useful method for understanding the differences among churches. The most obvious difference is in the process of ministerial placement. The appointment system of assigning ordained ministers to congregations that is used by Roman Catholics, Methodists, the Reorganized Church of Jesus Christ of Latter-day Saints, and a few other denominations, tends to encourage a degree of passivity among the laity that contrasts sharply with the more active stance of the laity in those churches where the members call their pastor. More important, however, is how differences in polity influence the decision-making processes. [8]

The emphasis on the office of the ruling elder in

30

Presbyterian churches, for example, appears to be one reason why Presbyterians have a remarkably large number of the laity actively involved in both denominational and interdenominational programs. By contrast, those denominations, such as the Lutherans and the Methodists, that have both a tradition and a polity designed to enhance the role of the clergy, do not enjoy the benefits of such strong lay participation.

If the focus is shifted from the denominational structures to the congregation, the influence of polity can be seen in many areas. Some denominations, such as the Anglicans, Episcopalians, Lutherans, and Presbyterians, have legitimized and institutionalized a system of representative church government that facilitates planning, decision-making, and the emergence of large congregations. Others, such as the Quakers, United Church of Christ, the Christian Church (Disciples of Christ), the Methodists, and the Church of the Brethren, have placed a far greater emphasis on participatory democracy. This tends to broaden the base of involvement, slow the decision-making process, encourage delay, and inhibit the emergence of large congregations.

The tremendous authority vested in the lay elders in the Reformed Church in America, the Christian Reformed Church, The Lutheran Church—Missouri Synod, and the several Presbyterian bodies has had the natural and predictable result of producing lay-clergy conflicts on doctrinal and biblical interpretation issues that rarely surface in other denominations that do not have the equivalent lay office with that degree of authority over the minister.

Many other examples could be cited to illustrate the importance of polity in understanding the internal dynamics of congregational life. One that has resurfaced again during the late 1970s and early 1980s reflects the differences in polity on the ownership of church property. In those denominations in which the congregation has absolute control over its real estate, it is much easier for a congregation to decide to sever its historic denominational affiliation than it is in those denominations where title to the property cannot be transferred without denominational approval. In other religious bodies the pension system has reinforced a sense of denominational loyalty among some of the clergy.

Perhaps most important of all, however, is the fact that the polity and size are the two most influential factors in shaping the role of the pastor and the relationship between the minister and the lay leaders.

10. *Role.* Another useful system for helping to understand the differences among churches is to classify them by role. One congregation, for example, sees its role primarily as a ministry to its members, while another places the primary emphasis on evangelizing among the unchurched. Or, one church seeks to serve recent newcomers to Toronto from Korea, while another sees its role as serving Lutherans with a strong Germanic heritage. In Grand Rapids one congregation sees it role as a ministry with persons from the very liberal left, while another defines its role as ministering to theologically conservative persons with strong ties to Holland. The new congregation may see its primary role as reaching unchurched newcomers to the community, while the eighty-year-old congregation a few miles away places a very high priority on reaching and retaining the teen-agers of member families.

Looking at churches in terms of a distinctive role is one of the most useful systems for classifying churches in order to discern the differences among congregations that otherwise may appear to be similar in terms of theological stance, interpretation of the Bible, denominational affiliation, age, size, community setting, polity, and the socio-economic status of the members.

Role is also important in planning and goal setting, in the operational definition of purpose, and in responding to some forms of passivity. Subsequent chapters in this volume place a very heavy emphasis on understanding the distinctive role of a congregation.

11. *Commitment.* In an informal fashion, one of the most widely used systems of classification for identifying the differences among congregations is illustrated by the comment, "The reason their church is growing and we're not is their members are more committed than we are." This approach has much to commend it, and it was the basis for the most influential book on American Protestantism published during the 1970s.[9] The basic difficulty with this approach is that some church members have a very strong commitment to Jesus Christ as Lord and Savior, while others have a very strong commitment to St. John's Church, and these two expressions of commitment have a less than one-hundred-percent overlap. Likewise, one member's strong commitment to the past and to the traditions developed in the past may conflict with another member's strong commitment to mission and outreach when the time comes to set priorities in the allocation of such scarce resources as people's time, energy, and talents. Unless it is defined more precisely (as Dean Kelley does when he uses the word "strict" to explain his thesis that the churches which project high expectations of their members tend to be growing churches), the use of this frame of reference for looking at churches usually creates more problems than it solves.

12. *Internal Dynamics.* In one of the most influential books ever written on the American presidency, James David Barber defined four types of presidential character. According to Barber, all Presidents fit into one of four categories: (1) active-positive (Washington, Franklin Roosevelt, Truman, and Kennedy), (2) active-negative (John Adams, Wilson, Hoover, Lyndon Johnson, and Nixon), (3) passive-positive (Jefferson, Taft, and Harding) and (4) passive-negative (Madison, Coolidge, and Eisenhower). Each type of personality follows a predictable behavior pattern.[10]

A parallel approach can be used in examining the internal dynamics of various congregations. Some congregations tend to drift into a state of passivity. Planning for ministry is more difficult in these passive churches than in the more active congregations. Some of the more common, but often subtle, symptoms of passivity are described in the next chapter.

In other words, the experiences of this writer strongly suggest that the active-passive distinction may be a very useful frame of reference for classifying congregations. This approach can be used to help both pastors and lay leaders diagnose what is happening in order to avoid counterproductive responses and to develop creative approaches to passivity. That is the central theme of this book. This volume is an attempt to identify the passive church as a distinct type of religious congregation and to suggest both diagnostic and prescriptive tools.

Another way of formulating the same basic concept can be developed by turning to the research and writing of Roger Barker and his colleagues. Barker's experiments have demonstrated that the environment or setting is a very significant variable that influences the behavior of individuals and groups.[11] The passive congregation constitutes a distinctive behavior setting that tends to produce certain types of predictable behavior among both the laity and the clergy. This behavior setting is very influential in determining the responses to the arrival of a new pastor, to the call for a reformulation of congregational priorities following the completion of a long building program, to the choice of the process to be used in redefining that congregation's role after the end of an era in its history, or to a debate over a proposed revision of the ministry with youth.

Passivity in a congregation, like asthma or leukemia or arthritis in an individual, produces some identifiable tendencies and behavior patterns that can be isolated, identified, described, and treated.

WHAT IS YOUR CLASSIFICATION SYSTEM?

That leads to the second major assumption on which this book is based. While some will regard this as excessively optimistic, it is a long-standing assumption of this writer that *people have a remarkable ability to respond creatively and productively to problems if they have the benefit of a reasonably accurate diagnosis of the situation.* In other words, whether the subject under consideration be personal, health care, parenting, church planning, responding to the changing seasons of the year, marital relationships, or politics, most people have a very high level of competence in dealing with the situation if they have the benefit of an accurate diagnosis of that slice of reality. This generalization is especially valuable when we can identify what we see happening as "normal and predictable behavior," given that particular set of circumstances. Most of us are reasonably comfortable and competent in responding to what we can identify as normal and predictable behavior. We tend to become uncomfortable and frustrated when we are faced with what we identify as strange, unpredictable, abnormal, or inexplicable behavior patterns. The residents of Grand Fork, North Dakota, for example, are less disturbed when the January temperature drops to 30° below zero than are the residents of Fort Lauderdale when the temperature dips to 25° above zero.

Most worshiping congregations drift into a period of passivity at one or more points in their life cycle. The leader, whether lay or ordained, who can recognize that as a normal and predictable pattern of institutional behavior will be more comfortable and competent in responding to that situation than will the individual who either cannot diagnose that condition or who is tempted to diagnose every passive congregation as "sick," "unfaithful," or "dying."

If the reader will pardon a bit of redundancy, the first major assumption on which this volume is based is that the system of classification used to look at churches will influence both the diagnosis and the prescription. The second major assumption is that, given the benefit of a reasonably accurate and relevant diagnosis of reality, most people have a remarkably high level of competence in responding to the conditions facing them.

The third major assumption takes the form of a warning that all too often the prescription produces the diagnosis. One example is the excessively large number of women who have undergone a radical mastectomy on the recommendation of a surgeon who was more comfortable with that treatment of breast cancer than with the use of chemotherapy. Another example is the church leader with a long background in the Sunday school, who recommends strengthening the Sunday church school as the solution for nearly all problems facing every congregation. A third illustration is the pastor who has developed skills in planning and financing building programs and, in every congregation he serves, leads that church into a building or major remodeling program. This volume is an attempt to describe a variety of congregational conditions, all of which represent, in one form or another, an expression of passivity in the church, and to suggest creative responses to passivity in the churches. Therefore, anyone reading beyond this page should be warned NOT to try to apply all of the diagnostic comments to every congregation or to classify every church as a passive parish. Just because the reader may feel comfortable with a particular prescription, it does not automatically follow that the church that the reader has in mind is a passive congregation! The suggestions on how to respond to passivity are appropriate only for use with passive congregations. They do not apply to all churches. Please do not try to make the diagnosis fit the prescription!

At this point some readers may be asking, Why use this elaborate set of different approaches to classifying churches in different categories? Why not simply act on the assumption that all congregations are called by the same Lord to the same mission? Why make life so complicated for the leaders, both lay and ordained, who have enough other things to worry about? This raises the fourth assumption on which this book rests.

It is assumed here that some leaders, regardless of whether they are ordained or lay, tend to be more effective in some situations and less effective in others. This generalization is illustrated by the physician who may recognize an asthmatic the first time the patient coughs, but may not be able to diagnose why the car will not start or why the physician's spouse is unhappy. The businessman who is very successful in directing a new business may be a failure when asked to become president of a stable, hundred-year-old family-owned corporation. The pastor who created a terrific record as the mission-developer of three different new congregations may have an unhappy experience when called to serve as the senior minister of a large, stable, and prestigious congregation. Not every reader will agree with Carl Dudley's statement that leadership is phase-oriented,[12] but there is more truth in that observation than many are willing to admit. One response to the concept of phase leadership is that a congregation looking for a new pastor might be well advised to seek a minister with the leadership style appropriate to that type of congregation at that point in its history. The same generalization applies to the enlistment and assignment of lay volunteers to policy-making positions.

Finally, it is assumed that while churches are different from one another, and no two are exactly alike, some do resemble one another, and congregational leaders can learn from the experiences of others. Some of the best learning comes from peers. Children may not learn as much from their father and mother as the parents would hope, but children do learn a lot from their peer group. Likewise, congregational leaders can learn from the experiences of others in similar churches. Unfortunately, however, the regional judicatories in most denominations are defined on the basis of geographical boundaries and/or for the convenience of the denomination, rather than to facilitate the cross-fertilization that could be encouraged by placing similar congregations in the same judicatory. One result is that the overwhelming majority of congregational leaders stay away from denominational training events planned on a regional basis. Some stay away because they are convinced the agenda is "not relevant to the particular needs of our unique situation."

One of the best responses to that behavior pattern is to encourage congregational leaders to go and spend a day or two with a church very similar to their own. Another, but less demanding, response is to give them a book such as this one in which the reader may identify with a situation described. This reader identification often produces a clearer understanding of *what* is happening in the reader's own congregation, *why* it is happening, and *how* to develop a creative alternative to what otherwise might be the normal institutional response.

Walter Brueggemann has said that "the task of the prophetic ministry is to nurture, nourish, and evoke a consciousness and perception alternative to the consciousness and perception of the dominant culture around us."[13]

In applying that concept to the passive church it is useful to recall Sir Isaac Newton's first law of motion; a body in motion tends to remain in motion and a body at rest tends to remain at rest.

The natural, predictable and normal response to passivity in the church tends to be to recreate the past by *maintaining the system*, "pushing the product,"[14] rebuilding the Sunday school, activating the inactive, filling the sanctuary, balancing the budget, maintaining the building, or attempting to replace the departed members with younger persons rather than to seek a genuine alternative to such institutional survival-oriented priorities.

The prophetic imagination will respond to passivity in a congregation by seeking a creative alternative to these efforts to recreate the past. One approach to discovering alternatives is to (1) recall the central elements of the heritage, (2) build on that heritage to identify new opportunities in ministry and to respond to the unmet needs of persons overlooked by most of the other churches in the community, (3) identify and mobilize the available resources, and (4) seek to affirm and build on the values and the heritage of the past *without feeling obligated to maintain in the same form all of the institutional apparatus, systems and structures inherited from the past.* Breaking the sequence of passivity in a congregation often requires finding new wineskins for the new wine (Mark 2:22). That is the responsibility of the prophetic imagination.

This discussion of a dozen different systems for classifying congregations and these five basic assumptions constitute the context for responding to the question, "What do you mean by that term, a passive church?"

CHAPTER TWO

WHAT IS A PASSIVE CHURCH?

"What do we do best as a congregation?" reflected Mary Kurtz as she pondered the question that had been asked her. This 47-year-old mother of three is one of the most active and knowledgeable members of the 485-member Central Church. After hesitating for several seconds she replied, "I guess if I were to brag about Central, the first thing I would mention is our choir. Two years ago we found a new choir director, and she has done a magnificent job of rebuilding the choir. A close second would be the sermon. Our new minister is not as flamboyant in his delivery as our previous pastor was, but he has a great deal more depth. Week after week, in a very quiet manner, he delivers some of the most powerful messages I've ever heard. As I think about it, I guess I would rank his preaching as the number one asset and put the chancel choir second on that list of what we do best here at Central Church. Third on that list, and I am sure there are many people who believe it is our number-one asset, is our youth program. Two years ago we hired a history teacher from the local high school and her husband to be our youth counselors. They are both mature adults, and with practically no help from anyone, except a couple of parents, they have built the best youth program we've ever had here. The junior high group has close to thirty kids in it, and the

senior high group averages between fifteen and twenty at
their meetings. I believe those are the three things we do best
as a congregation. Does that answer your question?"

"I don't know where this crazy scheme originated,"
declared Ben Harris, one of the most influential laymen and
a member of the board at Bethel Church, "but whoever
thought of it should have come to this board before
suggesting it to the kids. Does anyone have any idea of the
liability we would be exposing ourselves to if we let those kids
take a bus and go to Kentucky for a week?"

The subject under discussion at the board that Tuesday
evening in March was a proposal that two dozen of the high
school youth from Bethel Church would rent a bus, to be
driven by the adult counselors who would go along, for nine
days. The bus would be the vehicle to transport the youth for
a five-day work camp experience in one of the poverty-
stricken sections of Appalachia. The planning for the trip
had been underway since the previous September, and the
youth council was asking the board for approval of the
contract with the owner of the bus and with the insurance
company. Through a variety of work projects the members of
the youth group had raised the $5100 necessary to finance
the trip. They were not asking for money, only permission.
Since the bus rental contract and the insurance policy were
to be in the name of the church, they needed board approval.

"While the idea has a lot of merit, and I certainly want to
commend you kids for your concern for others and your
desire to be of service," added Steve Russo, "I have to go
along with Ben. I don't know enough about insurance to be
convinced this policy will cover all our potential liability,
and in good conscience I can't approve taking our
congregation out on a limb that someone else may saw off.
I'm afraid I'm going to have to vote against this proposal."

"Why do you kids have to go six hundred miles away to
find someone to help?" inquired Larry Harlow. "Can't you

find enough work projects to keep you busy right here in this community? There are dozens of widows living alone right here in this town who could use some help. When there's a world shortage of oil, why do you have to go so far away to find someone who needs your help?"

Fifteen minutes later, after more debate, seven months of planning by the youth was scuttled as the board voted 13 to 8 not to approve the two contracts. An hour and a half later, after the board had adjourned, Tommy Smith turned to Sally Turner and said, "Pretty soon we'll be known as the 'veto board.' Two months ago we vetoed the proposal by the women to have a bazaar, last month we turned down the pastor's proposal for a special visitation-evangelism program, and tonight we shot down the youth group's Appalachian trip and the Christian Education committee's recommendation that we create three new adult classes in the Sunday school."

"For some reason or other, but I don't know what it is, the enthusiasm here is at the lowest level I've ever seen it," complained 63-year-old Henry Churchill, a charter member of Faith Church. "This congregation dates back to the fall of 1952, and for years we saw ourselves as the most exciting church in this end of the county," he continued. "At first it was the glamor and excitement of pioneering a new church. We started out with only six families, but by the time we formally organized in January of 1953, we had 133 charter members. For a dozen years we were busy building a new congregation, a complete program, and the buildings to house it all. Those were exciting days!"

"They sure were!" agreed Sue Hankins. "Jim and I missed those first few years since we didn't get here until 1956, but one reason we picked Faith Church was because of the excitement in the air. There's a church of this same denomination about two miles closer to where we live, but some friends urged us to come here at least once, and after that first visit we knew this was the place for us," she reflected with obvious nostalgia in her voice. "But the middle sixties also were good years here," she added. "That's when we first began to get involved in a lot more community outreach. Jim Davis came as our third pastor in 1963, and he was the key figure. Jim was far more interested in community outreach than in building buildings. It was under his leadership that we started Mother's Day Out, the weekday nursery school, the Adult Forum in the Sunday School, the annual day of fasting for world hunger, Meals on Wheels, the Golden Age Club, and the annual work camp-mission tour for the high school kids."

"Those were pretty exciting years," added Bob Romano, who was starting his twenty-second year as the treasurer of Faith Church. "But it was also under Jim Davis that we reached our peak and began our decline. Jim also was the one who scrapped the plans to build the permanent sanctuary. He was the one who proposed remodeling the fellowship hall, which was intended to be used for worship for only a few years when it was built, into a permanent worship facility. He repeatedly said that he was more interested in being pastor of a vital congregation than in building a big congregation."

"That's right," agreed Betty Phillips. "We were averaging close to 325 at worship right after Jim arrived, following those disastrous two years with Reverend Johnson. I was on the committee that studied the whole issue of building a permanent sanctuary back in 1968. My husband and I had been here only a couple of years at the time and I realized my voice didn't carry much weight against the pastor's, but I was one of those who opposed Jim Davis on that. I wanted to go ahead and build the permanent sanctuary that was a part of the original master plan. We could have done it back in 1968 for less than a third of what it would cost today. But, just as you say, Sue, Jim Davis was not much for building buildings. He preferred to be active out in the community so we didn't build it."

"Maybe it's just as well we didn't build it," observed Ira Newman. "By the time Jim left in 1973, we were down to about 70 at the first service and 125 at the second. The remodeled fellowship hall will seat close to 220, including the choir, so I guess we don't need a bigger building."

"That's a misreading of history, Ira," corrected Bob Romano, the church treasurer. "If Jim Davis had worked as hard as our first pastor did in bringing in new members, instead of spending so much time out in the community, we could be averaging over four hundred at worship on Sunday morning. That would give us twice the income we have now. We could be paying $60,000 or $70,000 a year on a mortgage and still have more for local expenses and benevolences than we have now. In fact, if we had gone ahead and built the new sanctuary back in 1968, we probably would have it all paid for by now!"

"This sounds more like a meeting to do a post mortem on the past than the first meeting of a long range planning committee," interrupted Alan Hamilton who had been sitting silently while listening to the discussion. "I joined this congregation while Jim Davis was the pastor here," he continued. "In fact, Jim Davis was the major reason my wife and I picked this church. Like Sue, we live closer to two other churches of this denomination than we do this building, but we chose this because of Jim Davis, and we're glad we did. As Henry and Sue pointed out, this isn't the exciting place it used to be, but we still like it here."

"Maybe that should be the first thing this committee looks at," suggested Helen Taylor. "I've been a member here for over twenty years now, and I have to agree it's not as exciting as it used to be. In fact, I would go a couple of steps farther and suggest this is a complacent, passive, self-satisfied, and overly comfortable bunch of people."

"I may look like I'm comfortable and complacent," retorted Henry Churchill, "but I'm not. Don't let my gray hair fool you! I won't be satisfied until we go back to one worship service on Sunday morning. That's the basic reason why Betty and I both favored building the new sanctuary back in 1968. We both served on that special committee, and if we had had stronger ministerial leadership, we would have built it! Now it's too late, I guess, because building costs have skyrocketed, but we could still go a long way toward uniting this congregation by having only one worship service. Ira, you just said we now have a combined average attendance of 195 and can seat 200. We don't need two services, if we can get everybody in at one service!"

"Wait a minute, Henry," replied Alan Hamilton, "if we cut back to one service, our attendance will drop to 160 or 170. One of the reasons it's as high as it is today is because we offer people the choice of two different hours. Cut it back to one and our attendance will drop by 15 to 20 percent."

"This congregation was spoiled by having only two pastors during its first eighty-three years," explained Helen Schroeder. "Dr. Otto Schultz was the founding pastor back in 1892. He retired in 1943 and was followed by Dr. Donald Becker, who retired in 1975. I've been a member here at Grace Church for over fifty years, and I knew them both very well. They were typical first-born children, and they were both very strong leaders. They told us what needed to be done and we did it. Dr. Schultz was probably the better pastor and Dr. Becker was certainly the better preacher, but both of them were pretty authoritarian in terms of a leadership style. They both loved this parish and the people responded. The pastor was the parent and the members were the children.

"When Dr. Becker retired in 1975, he was followed by Reverend Olson who resigned a few months ago. Reverend Olson is a good preacher and an excellent pastor, but he is thirty years younger than Dr. Becker and not at all as aggressive. In fact, I believe that in psychological terms, he would be classified as an introvert. I'm one of two women on the pulpit search committee, and I believe we need a more aggressive leader. Today our worship attendance is about half what it was back in 1970, and our Sunday school attendance is less than a fourth of what it was at its peak back in the early 1960s. We need a strong leader."

"That's exactly the way I see it," agreed Hank Erickson, a big, burly, hard-driving 60-year-old businessman who chaired the search committee at Grace Church. "Ever since Dr. Becker announced he was going to retire, I've argued that we need to find a preacher who can draw the crowds. We need a minister who is a dynamic preacher, a great mixer and a man who can get out into the community where people can meet him. In a downtown church like this we need a minister who is a joiner, who likes to get out and meet people. Old Doc Becker was that kind of person. He was a member of the Kiwanis Club, the Chamber of Commerce, the Briarwood Country Club and a dozen other organizations and clubs. Everybody in town knew him, and he knew everybody. That's why Grace Church reached its peak during those years. Becker's personality and his preaching are what filled this church. A few years before he retired, he told me that the previous year he had had 135 funerals, two-thirds of them for non-members. He was the right man for this church, and this church will continue to decline until we get a dynamic preacher like Becker who can draw crowds and fill this place Sunday after Sunday."

"I'm intrigued that you keep referring to this super-preacher as a man, Hank. Don't you think we ought to consider a woman minister?" asked Diane Spring, a 33-year-old member of nine years who represented the new-member element on the pulpit search committee at Grace Church.

"Are you crazy?" retorted Hank Erickson. "I have nothing against women in the ministry and I think we might consider one when we start looking for a new associate, but it would take a man to do what needs to be done here to restore Grace Church to its proper place in this city!"

These four examples illustrate several of the basic characteristics of the passive church. Each situation illustrates some of the attitudes, conditions and historical content that can be found in hundreds of what have become passive congregations. In each one of these four congregations passivity has replaced enthusiasm, divisiveness has replaced a sense of unity, goallessness has replaced an emphasis on specific goals, and drift has replaced a sense of direction.

How Did It Happen?

Perhaps the best beginning point in offering a description of the passive church is to review what happened in each of the four congregations described here.

In the first example, Mary Kurtz identified the sermon, the chancel choir and the youth program as the strongest components of the total ministry of Central Church.

The basic responsibility for each one is placed on a paid staff member. This is one of the most common signs of the passive church. The congregation employs a staff member to carry out the major ministries of the church. That enables the vast majority of the adults to enjoy a relatively passive role listening to those inspiring sermons and that wonderful choir while paid staff members do most of the work.

While it is easy to underestimate the value of program staff in a church, and too many churches are staffed for decline rather than for growth, one of the basic causes of passivity in many congregations is the "Let's hire it done" syndrome.

In the second example, the board at Bethel Church illustrated one of the basic axioms of life. People tend to enjoy doing what they have had considerable practice doing.

As Tommy Smith observed at the close of the meeting, this had become a "veto board."

It is relatively easy for a congregation's governing body to drift into a permission-withholding stance when ideas for new ministries and new programs are proposed. This posture tends to inhibit the creativity of the members, to halt the flow of innovative suggestions from individuals and program committees, and to encourage passivity. After years of experience vetoing a variety of proposals and suggestions, the board at Bethel Church practiced what it knew how to do.

The third example illustrates four of the most common sources of passivity in a congregation. In its early days Faith Church illustrated the value of broad-based and widely supported goals in providing a sense of direction and movement in a congregation—and also what happens when that broad-based support begins to dissolve. Faith Church was filled with active excitement as the members pioneered the creation of a new congregation and rallied together in supporting the specific, attainable, measurable, visible, unifying, exciting, and rewarding goal of constructing a new meeting place. For some members that original goal was replaced by a new definition of purpose under the direction of the Reverend Jim Davis. The new rallying point was a greater emphasis on community outreach, but that new priority did not gain the broad-based support that had been accorded the building program. The resulting division over priorities encouraged passivity.

Another source of passivity illustrated by the experiences at Faith Church is the price of looking backward. For close to two decades this was a congregation in which the members' attention was directed toward today and tomorrow, first in organizing a new congregation, expanding the program, and constructing a meeting house, and subsequently in expanding the community outreach of the congregation. Today it appears that more effort is being devoted to looking backward and second-guessing the past. That tends to be one of the most fertile sources of passivity.

A third, and one of the most subtle sources of passivity illustrated by the course of events at Faith Church is that when the distinctive role of a church begins to be eroded, it becomes increasingly difficult to agree on goals, and before long that state of goallessness breeds passivity.

Faith Church began back in 1952 with a clearly defined role as a new mission. This role was reinforced by the goals of reaching prospective members, becoming financially self-supporting, developing and expanding programs, planning and completing a couple of building programs, reaching more people, and reducing its indebtedness. Eleven years later, as that role began to wear a little thin, Jim Davis arrived as the third pastor and aggressively promoted a new role as a community outreach-oriented parish. A series of goals, including the weekday nursery school, the Mother's Day Out program, the Golden Age Club, Meals on Wheels, World Hunger, and the work camp experience for youth were adopted to reinforce that new role. While the growth curve leveled off and began to decline during that era, everyone agrees that was a very active and exciting era in the history of Faith Church. It appears that when Jim Davis left in 1973, much of the support for this second role evaporated, and Faith Church needed to define a new role for itself to provide the context for a third era of productive goal setting. Since role takes precedence over goals, it was necessary to redefine the role of Faith Church following Jim Davis's departure before goals could be formulated to reinforce that new role. When this did not happen, the enthusiasm began to fade and the congregation drifted into an era of gradual decline. Today, institutional maintenance appears to be moving to the top of the priority list at Faith Church. This sequence of moving from a clearly defined role, supported by a series of compatible, satisfaction-producing, and reinforcing goals, to a new role, again with a set of compatible and reinforcing goals for that role, to an era when the agreement on a sense of distinctive purpose has largely dissolved, is a common source of passivity in churches. When institutional maintenance replaces ministry as the top priority, passivity often is not far behind!

A fourth source of passivity, illustrated by the experiences of Faith Church, overlaps the other three. This is confusion over the criteria for congregational self-evaluation. For more than a decade the morale and self-image at Faith Church were reinforced by favorable reports on the two highly visible and easy-to-measure yardsticks for self-evaluation. One was numerical growth in the size of the congregation. The other was progress in constructing "our own meeting place." When the basic role was redefined as community outreach, the criteria for self-evaluation changed (for some members, but not all!) to new programs in community outreach. While these criteria were more subjective and did not win a universal base of support, they did provide a sense of satisfaction, a feeling of progress, and a belief in accomplishment for those supportive of the new role.

Today, however, it appears there is a divisive lack of agreement on the appropriate criteria for self-evaluation. Should these include completion of the original master plan for construction of a permanent sanctuary? Reversing the decline in numerical growth? Achieving the earlier goal of having everyone worship together in one service on Sunday morning? Increasing the dollar receipts of the congregation? Staying out of debt? Reinforcing and expanding the outreach into the community? Agreeing on the identity of a scapegoat for the change in direction? Restoring the sense of excitement, progress, and movement that marked the first decades of Faith Church's history?

When there is a lack of agreement on the criteria for congregational self-evaluation, it becomes very easy for a congregation to drift into a state of complacency and passivity.

Another common source of passivity in a congregation is illustrated by what happened at Grace Church following the end of Dr. Becker's thirty-two-year pastorate. When a congregation's role and community image is built around the personality and talents of one minister for two, three, or four decades, a huge gap is created when that minister leaves the scene. Occasionally that void is filled, as Hank Erickson wants it to be at Grace Church, by the arrival of a new "superpreacher." More often, the departure of that dominant pulpit figure is followed by (a) the relatively brief pastorate of the successor who frequently turns out to be (unintentionally) an interim pastor and (b) a long period of passivity before the congregation is able to develop and project into the community a new self image and retrain the lay leadership to function with a different style of ministerial leadership.

The four brief case studies offered at the beginning of this chapter are presented partly to illustrate the nature of the passive church and partly to help the reader identify some of the more common sources of passivity. Before moving on to describe a self-analysis tool for determining the degree of passivity in a congregation, it may be useful to summarize some of the major sources of passivity.

What Are the Sources?

While it is impossible to demonstrate an absolute cause and effect relationship, it is possible to identify what appear to be several of the most common sources for congregational passivity. A review of these causes can be used, not only in diagnosing this syndrome, but more important, in developing a prescription for renewal. One of the basic assumptions behind the preparation of this book is that if an accurate diagnosis can be made of the situation, it is relatively easy to develop the appropriate prescription.

1. Perhaps the most common source of passivity in a

congregation is the effect of the sense of mission's being eroded and replaced by a priority on institutional self-preservation. Many of the members intuitively feel this is incompatible with the basic nature of a Christian congregation, and they begin to lose interest.

2. A parallel pattern can be identified in those congregations in which there is a comparatively limited programmatic emphasis on evangelism, education, nurture, missions, or widespread involvement in community ministries.

Perhaps the simplest means of identifying this pattern is by a single question. Where do the outstanding lay volunteers serve as leaders? On the finance committee, as trustees, on the governing board and on the personnel committee? Or as teachers, on the evangelism committee, as greeters, on the missions committee, as callers on the worship committee, and in the choir?

3. Another common cause of passivity is the orientation toward today and tomorrow gradually being replaced with an increasingly strong orientation toward the past. Sometimes this takes the form of glorying in "the good old days." Occasionally it is expressed in the search for a scapegoat from yesterday who can be held responsible for today's problems.

This past orientation is often reinforced when many of the current leaders have been in office for at least a decade, and some have been leaders for more than twenty years. While there are many exceptions to this generalization, the pattern of normal and predictable human behavior is that the older the person, and/or the longer that individual has been in the same office or position of leadership, the stronger the past orientation. The natural stance of long-term leaders is to look toward the past rather than the future—partly because they have had years and years of experience with the past.

4. A significant, but less common, cause of congregational passivity is some of the dreams held by many of the long-time members not being fulfilled, resulting in frustration which may dominate all discussions, regardless of

the formal agenda. The "unfulfilled dream" is often a synonym for passivity.

5. Another major cause of passivity is building the most highly visible and satisfying components of the total package of ministry around the performance of paid staff members. This was the situation Mary Kurtz described at Central Church, where preaching, the choir, and the youth program dominated the agenda.

6. The departure of the long-tenured pastor from the minister-centered church is often an obvious cause of passivity. It becomes especially difficult to counter when that condition is combined with the selection of a cadre of lay leaders who also carry a heavy workload in their profession or vocation and have limited time and energy left for their congregational responsibilities. They do have the time to talk, but lack the energy to act. When the "superpreacher" leaves—and eventually everyone does—the congregation is left with a corps of articulate and high-powered followers, but with few initiators who possess the creativity to redefine the role of that congregation, and who also have the discretionary time and energy to help implement a new direction. Grace Church and Hank Erickson illustrate that combination.

One of the most widely shared misconceptions is that the congregation that includes a large number of members who are energetic, articulate, highly educated, and hard-working business leaders and professionals (attorneys, physicians, teachers, engineers, et al.) has a tremendous resource of creative, highly skilled, aggressive, and experienced leaders. Frequently that is not true, and the minister and other members often wonder why.

One part of the answer has been supplied by Pierre Mornell and his research on "the passive male."[1] Dr. Mornell, a psychiatrist who has specialized in marriage counseling, contends that many men who are very active, articulate, energetic, and successful in their work come home at night and are inactive, inarticulate, lethargic, withdrawn, and passive in their relationships with their wives. When the husband comes home from a stress-filled and active day at work that has been overloaded with problem-solving challenges, he is ready to "tune out." He is not seeking the stress that often goes with a room full of people. He is not seeking conflict. He is not seeking new challenges. He is not seeking the "opportunity" to solve someone else's problems. He is looking for peace, quiet, privacy, and the opportunity to relax.

His wife, who may have been at home all day, is often ready for conversation, company, excitement, and activity. Her husband is not. Dr. Mornell suggests this active wife–passive husband syndrome may be a major factor behind the soaring divorce rate in recent years.

It is not difficult to translate Dr. Mornell's frame of reference to the monthly board meeting at First Church. The recently arrived pastor, who never before served a congregation with so many high-powered lay leaders, has spent much of the day preparing for this evening and is looking forward to an active, creative, challenging, and enjoyable two hours of problem solving. At the appropriate time, the pastor, who is still perceived by most members as our "new minister," asks, "Now what do you folks believe we should define as our top priorities in ministry for the coming year?"

Seven of the eight men and four of the six women on the board have just come from a "hard day at the office," gulped a hasty supper and hurried over to the church for the board meeting. They are prepared to be more or less passive evaluators and affirmers of what the pastor will be proposing. After all, that is the role the previous pastor had spent a couple of decades training the board for and what they are comfortable doing. During most of the two-hour meeting that evening ten of the board members passively watch and listen as the new minister and three or four board members discuss priorities for the coming year.

Late that night the minister goes home, following two hours of normal and predictable behavior by two-thirds of the board members, and says to his wife, "I simply can't understand why a bunch of remarkably gifted, highly trained, exceptionally competent, and obviously brilliant board members can sit there like a bunch of dummies for two hours at a board meeting! I never expected *this* to be a passive church!"

7. A parallel pattern of passivity sometimes is found in the congregation in which the historical record reveals either a high turnover in ministers and program staff members, and/or the strong-willed and authoritarian leadership style of one staff person who served for a long period ot time. Frequently the dominating leadership style, abrasive personality, and long tenure of this staff person (minister, church secretary, choir director, organist, associate minister, or director of Christian Education) has caused some members to leave, others to drop into inactivity, and many potential new leaders never to join because of this one staff person. The passive stance is the most comfortable response for most of the laity.

8. A comparatively widespread cause of congregational passivity is soliciting ideas, suggestions, complaints, recommendations and criticisms from all the members with great publicity—and then (a) ignoring all this material or (b) digesting it, but never reporting back to the members on what happened or (c) vetoing all or nearly all proposals for innovative programming. Ben Harris and his colleagues at Bethel Church illustrated this syndrome.

9. One of the most complex sources of passivity in a congregation can be traced back to a decline in the numerical size of the church. There are at least four comon dimensions to this condition. First, the declining church usually is receiving *and assimilating* a comparatively small

number of new members. Since new members often constitute the major source of new ideas, enthusiasm, a strong and optimistic view of the future, creative and productive workers for new ventures, and support for the current minister, the lack of a flood of new members often creates a favorable climate for passivity.

Second, the organization that has been growing in size for many years usually displays considerable tolerance for deviation from traditional norms, for venturesome and future-oriented leaders, for creativity, for innovation and for risk-taking. When that organization begins to shrink in size, it often tends to become less open to deviations from traditional norms, less supportive of the venturesome and future-oriented leader, less capable of offsetting or nullifying the impact of incompetent leaders or office-holders, and more inclined to "choose up sides" than to support innovative proposals. A common response to what may come to be perceived as divisive conflict is passivity.

A third dimension of this source of passivity is that the shrinking organization tends to place institutional maintenance at the top of the priority list, and that tends to repel the more venturesome persons and to attract the passive personality. Finally, when an organization begins to decline in size, there often follows the temptation to attempt to "do yesterday" once again. This also tends to repel the more creative, future-oriented, and enthusiastic potential new adherents who could help chart a new course of action.

10. A less obvious, but widespread, cause of passivity is the completion of a "chapter" in the congregation's history—such as the end of a long and effective pastorate, relocation to a new meeting place, inaugurating a new dimension of ministry, completion of that original three-stage building plan of twenty-five years ago, or the healing of a divisive split—when the congregation has not been able to project to non-members a distinctive identity or community image beyond this now-completed goal. The lack of this

clear identity inhibits the evangelistic outreach, reinforces the low self-esteem, undercuts enthusiasm, and is both a cause and a reflection of passivity.

11. One of the more destructive causes of passivity is a long history of divisive and unresolved conflict that has caused a disproportionately large number of members to stay away or to simply drop out.

For the vast majority of adults the most attractive response to conflict is to walk away from it. Some church members respond to conflict by changing congregations, many more simply drift into a passive stance on the sidelines, and a few enjoy active participation.

12. A similar result may follow if the past decade has been filled with a series of relatively minor, but numerous, anxiety-producing experiences that caused some members to drop out because they prefer to avoid conflict or cannot cope with anxiety.

13. One of the more common causes of passivity is the widespread feeling among the members that they have been rejected by one or more of the previous pastors. This is especially common among those congregations that usually are served by a minister who (a) served that congregation while in school and left following graduation, (b) came directly from seminary and left for a larger congregation after a few years of experience in that first pastorate, or (c) left the parish ministry to accept a "promotion" to a bureaucratic office in the denominational structure. Sometimes the members refer to their congregation as an apprenticeship church or as a stepping-stone, in an effort to explain the passivity.

14. Another common cause of passivity, similar to the last item, is a series of short pastorates. This often causes the congregation to develop a high level of competence in three areas: (a) giving parties to welcome the new minister, (b) watching the new minister get acquainted with the people

and with that parish, (c) giving parties to bid farewell to the departing minister.

15. A frequently overlooked major cause of congregational passivity is limited opportunities for corporate worship. Frequently this includes a shift, or a proposed shift, from two worship services on Sunday morning to one. The goal of fellowship and of functioning as "one big happy family" has replaced the preaching of the Word and the administration of the sacraments as the basic reason for being.

16. One of the more subtle causes of congregational passivity is the tendency of every organization to exploit people on behalf of a cause or for the operation of their organization. A common example of this in the churches is asking adult volunteers to teach in the children's division— and then scheduling the Sunday school so the teachers can rarely participate in corporate worship. Another example is to overload eager young new members with jobs until they "burn out."

17. While it is comparatively rare, an interesting source of passivity is the "tenant church syndrome." This condition may be found in some of those congregations that do not hold title to their meeting place, do not intend to build, and do not feel under any pressure to have their own meeting place. Sometimes it is a small inner city congregation that has lost its meeting place because of a fire and believes it cannot rebuild. Sometimes it is a large and comparatively well-to-do congregation meeting in a university student center. Occasionally it is a long-established congregation meeting in the auditorium at a denominationally operated camp or retreat site. Or, it may be the congregation that is "renting," for a nominal amount of money, the building that is owned and jointly used by another congregation of a different denomination. Tenant congregations tend to be passive, to develop a dependency stance, to become excessively dependent on paid staff and a very small cadre of

lay volunteers, to develop a below-average level of financial support, to display a below-average level of member commitment, to have difficulty reaching "a new generation" of leaders, and to drift toward a relatively narrow leadership base. The tenant church often drifts gradually toward passivity.

18. Another subtle source of passivity can be, in some middle-sized and larger congregations, few members knowing more than a small proportion of the total membership by name. This tends to be a serious concern when most of the long-time leaders cannot address the newer members by name. Since many of the most creative suggestions for innovative ministries come from newer members, this high level of anonymity tends to smother activity and nourish passivity.

19. While one must be cautious about exaggerating the cause-and-effect relationship, there is a pronounced tendency toward an excessive degree of passivity in those congregations in which substantially more than one-half of the adult (age eighteen and over) members have been in that same congregation for twelve to fifteen years or longer, and are older couples with no children under eighteen at home, widowed, or never-married mature adults. This reinforces the feeling that "we have done our share of work here."

20. Again it is difficult to prove a cause-and-effect relationship, but an excessive degree of passivity tends to be found in those congregations in which (a) there is a lack of a consistent and continuing emphasis on opportunities for personal and spiritual growth for adults, (b) there is a comparatively low level of competence in the members, and especially the leaders, in articulating their faith, (this characteristic often is reinforced by the lack of any programmatic emphasis to help people develop this ability), (c) there is a conspicuous lack of any systematic and continuing program of lay leadership development, (d) there are relatively few large group fellowship and social events

designed to decrease the level of anonymity among the members, and (e) almost the entire responsibility for the evangelistic outreach of the congregation and for the operation of the new member recruitment system has been delegated to paid staff members.

21. Two of the most interesting, and not uncommon, sources of passivity in churches can be traced back to the anticipated departure of a minister or to the arrival of a new pastor.

The first expression of this phenomenon begins to emerge when the long-term pastor announces, *several years in advance*, that his retirement date is now visible on the horizon. Sometimes the announcement is vague in content, informal in nature, and without a fixed date. The minister makes the members aware of his impending retirement by the repeated references to "growing old," to "retirement is not far away now," and to "before long you'll be getting along without me here in this great church." The members interpret this as the foundation for the formal announcement that will follow with a fixed date for retirement. When the formal announcement is not made, the people drift into a passive stage of waiting.

In its most destructive form this syndrome includes the reference to what is perceived as a fixed date, but when that day begins to draw near, the references are changed to a later date. The empire-builder is reluctant to surrender control of his empire, and the members, as they grow weary of trying to keep track of that moving target, simply surrender.

In other cases, the minister, who fears that the rising tide of discontent with his ministry may produce a crisis before that retirement date is reached, immobilizes the congregation by a formal announcement with a stated date, but that date is three or four years down the road. In retrospect three years may appear to be a very brief span of time, but living through the final three years of an increasingly unpopular or ineffective pastorate may seem like an eternity to lay persons, who often choose the easier road of adopting a passive stance.

Another expression of what is basically the same syndrome can often be observed when the very talented, extremely personable, highly articulate, unusually creative, and remarkably attractive minister arrives on the scene following the traumatic final years of a disastrous pastorate. Instead of being greeted by a large corps of enthusiastic lay persons ready and eager to begin work on carving out a new and exciting chapter in the history of this congregation, just as the pulpit nominating committee had promised, the new minister finds the resulting euphoria has generated a new form of passivity. The unhappy and passive congregation of yesterday has become the euphoric and passive congregation of today!

22. One of the most interesting causes of passivity is the existence of a network of criteria for self-evaluation that causes the members to view this congregation as small, weak, inept, unfaithful, unsuccessful, dull, uninteresting, dying, or without a future. The result often is a low self-image, a sense of powerlessness, defeatism, and passivity. The amazing dimension of this cause of passivity is that many of these counterproductive criteria for self-evaluation have been created by highly educated clergy and denominational leaders.

23. One of the most difficult-to-counter causes of passivity is the widespread feeling of powerlessness and the belief that "someone else controls our destiny." In the denominations in which ministers are appointed, rather than called, this "someone else" may be identified as the denominational officials charged with ministerial placement. In the 1950s many rural and small town churches identified the rural-to-urban migration of young adults as the force that undercut their life. A few years later, the members of hundreds of city churches referred to "the changing neighborhood" as the factor that wiped out their ability to plan for the future. During the late 1970s and early 1980s,

inflation was perceived as the force that shaped events, but was beyond the control of the membership. Each of these developments nurtured passivity.

24. Many congregations, frequently motivated by guilt over the ownership of a sparsely-used building, have drifted into the "landlord role." The leaders, sometimes over the opposition of a substantial number of members, decide to encourage a variety of community groups and organizations to use the church building to house their offices and/or programs. A frequent result is a "busy building" and a passive congregation.[2]

The members are able to rationalize their continued existence as a congregation by explaining they are "doing good" by making their meeting place available to community groups, but few if any members may be actively involved in these programs or agencies.

25. One of the major causes of passivity may be the completion of a goal-oriented era. The goals that were identified earlier either have been accomplished or have been scrapped. Since role takes precedence over goals,[3] it is difficult, and frequently impossible, for the members to agree on a new set of goals until a new role has been defined. Until this redefinition of role has been accomplished, the congregation tends to drift passively without a sense of direction. This was one of the sources of passivity illustrated by Faith Church.

26. The parallel to this source of passivity is the completion of a major, long-term, means-to-an-end, congregational goal. Three common examples of this are (a) the creation of a new congregation and its first ten or twelve years of building programs, (b) the relocation to a new site and construction of a new meeting place on that site, and (c) making the final payments on a fifteen- or twenty-year mortgage. These are *not* ministry goals, they are only means-to-an-end goals. Fulfillment of this type of goal is often followed by a period of passivity.

WHAT IS A PASSIVE CHURCH?

27. One of the two or three most effective means of creating passivity in a congregation is to use guilt as the basic motivating force. While this may enable the congregation to achieve ambitious goals and it often produces a large amount of superficial activity, eventually it takes its toll. The Christian Church is based on the love of God for His children and the use of guilt as a motivating tool runs counter to that basic theme. In some congregations it may take a generation for the full sequence to become visible, but guilt usually leads first to agitated activity followed by hostility and finally by passivity.

What is the value in identifying such a long list of the sources of passivity in a congregation? There are at least three reasons why the concerned church leader may find it useful to review such a list.

First, there is the obvious relief and reassurance in being able to identify the general context for looking at a specific concern. The new mother, for example, who is feeling emotionally depressed, gains reassurance when she discovers that many new mothers experience what is sometimes described as postpartum blues. The parent who begins to feel anxious and rejected when the seventeen-year-old son begins to make daily references to how many days remain before high school graduation and the day he is free to leave home, regains some degree of self-esteem after discovering that the parents of other high school seniors also are being subjected to similar countdowns! The congregational leader, who has become convinced this particular congregation is suffering from a unique, and probably fatal case of passivity, may be relieved to discover that the problem is so widespread that it can be identified as a common pattern—and there are at least twenty-seven different varieties of the problem! Identifying the pain as a normal, predictable, and widespread problem does not automatically produce a solution, but it does free some people to be able to examine alternative courses of action.

63

A second, and by far the most important, reason for looking at this variety of sources of passivity is illustrated by a story told by Martin J. Heimlich, M.D., the originator of the famous Heimlich Maneuver. Several years ago he published an article describing how a lay person, by the use of a simple bear hug, could save the life of an individual who was choking to death on a piece of food. The article was published in the June 1974 issue of *Emergency Medicine*. That same month, at a medical dinner meeting in Washington, D.C., a physician choked to death on a chunk of food while a hundred physicians stood by helplessly.

In reflecting on that episode, Dr. Heimlich observed, "The diagnosis of choking on food had been left so complex that even a large group of physicians failed to recognize the tragedy occurring in their midst."[4] Subsequently Dr. Heimlich concluded that if his solution to the problem was going to have widespread application, it would be necessary to break down a complex situation into a simple and easily recognized sequence so a lay person could recognize what was wrong and begin to take remedial action. That meant articulating a simple step-by-step diagnostic procedure that would enable anyone—including persons with absolutely no medical training, such as a parent or a person sitting across the table from the victim—to recognize the symptoms and complete the Heimlich Maneuver within three or four minutes. Dr. Heimlich identified the three-step sequence of choking on food, as distinct from a stroke or a heart attack or some other affliction, as (1) the person cannot breathe and *cannot speak*, (2) the person turns blue and (3) the person falls unconscious. When *all three* of these symptoms are present, it is safe to assume that person is choking on a chunk of food and will die within four minutes unless remedial action is taken.[5] Thanks to Dr. Heimlich's efforts, nearly one thousand lives are saved every year.

The parallel here is reasonably obvious, although perhaps somewhat presumptuous. On any given day thousands of ministers and hundreds of thousands of the laity experience varying degrees of frustration because the congregation of which they are members does not display the vitality, the sense of mission, the joy, the concern for persons outside the membership, the enthusiasm, and the vigor that is presumed to be a part of the ongoing life of a called-out community of the followers of Jesus Christ. They feel the passivity of that congregation has deafened the members to the call of the Lord. How can they respond to this stifling passivity?

One response is to leave. That is a course of action chosen by countless ministers and thousands of lay persons every year.

Another alternative is to stand by helplessly and watch what happens to be the gradual decline and eventual death of that church.

A third possibility is to call an expert in to help with the diagnosis, prognosis, prescription, and definition of alternative courses of action. That is not a particularly attractive possibility, however, since most congregations have an earned skepticism about the potential contributions of any outside, third-party, parish consultant. They are reluctant to turn to outside "experts" until the passage of time has greatly reduced the number of attractive courses of action.

Another alternative, and the central theme of this chapter, is to break the complex nature of the passive church down into a series of symptoms or sources so that anyone can recognize them and say, "Aha! Now I see what is happening, and I can understand why it is happening." That big "Aha!" is the first step in an effective response to any problem, whether it be a person choking to death on a piece of meat, the gradual deterioration of the governing body of a congregation into a "veto board," the "post- building blues" that often follows the completion of an exciting building program, or the passivity of the typical tenant church.

In addition to helping the reader identify with a normal and predictable pattern of congregational behavior and look behind the symptoms to discover the sources of the problem, there is a third value in examining this long list of the sources of passivity. This can be seen by looking at the sequence of diagnosis → prescription → action. Only if there is an accurate diagnosis of the basic cause or sources of passivity in a congregation will it be possible to choose the appropriate response. The central thesis of this book is that the most productive response to passivity in a congregation is to identify the sources of the passivity and choose the response that matches the cause or sources. If they have the benefit of an accurate diagnosis, most congregational leaders will be able to choose the appropriate course of action to combat passivity. Before looking at one prescription that is the best response to several forms of passivity, however, it may be useful to review a brief checklist that can be used in identifying the symptoms of passivity.

A Checklist for Self-Appraisal

An overlapping and supplemental approach to identifying the symptoms and the common characteristics of the passive church is to use a checklist. Since not all of the items on such a checklist have equal weight, it may be useful to assign points to each symptom. Check each of these characteristics that applies to your congregation, and note the points assigned in parentheses to that item. When you finish checking the symptoms that apply to your congregation, add up the number of points accumulated, and compare it with the scale that follows this checklist.

1. The most obvious characteristic, and certainly one of the most serious that mark the passive church, is the low level of self-esteem. This low level of congregational self-esteem is a major factor behind the lack of enthusiasm and the apparent complacency. In simple terms, there is the lack of a justifiable and healthy pride in what is happening in ministry and program *today*. (10)

2. The physical care of the building is below average and often conveys to the visitor a We-don't-care attitude. (4)

3. There is a heavy dependence on the pastor and/or paid staff to take initiative and give direction. (5)

4. There is a strong past-orientation *and* a widespread feeling that the "best days" of this congregation are clearly in the past. (8)

5. More than one-half of today's members have been members of this congregation for twelve years or longer. (5)

6. There is a lack of anything resembling evangelical fervor. (10)

7. Today's congregation is smaller than it was at its peak. (4)

8. The policy-makers tend to be drawn largely from among those persons who were members when the congregation was at or near its peak and who have first-hand recollections of "the good old days." (7)

9. A comparatively large proportion of today's members are relatively inactive. (8)

10. The focus of the program is largely on music, children and youth, therefore most of the adults remain in a relatively passive role. (9)

11. When the leaders discuss priorities in the allocation of resources, there is a widespread tendency to emphasize the conservation of time, energy, money, and physical facilities and to talk in terms of either-or rather than both-and. (5)

12. "Efficiency and economy" are more important considerations in decision-making than performance and relationships. (5)

13. The quality of internal communication between the congregation as a whole and the individual members is usually less than adequate and is often inaccurate, confusing, and incomplete. (A common example is that one announcement states the beginning time for a special event is 2 P.M. while another places it at 1:30 P.M.) (6)

14. There is a very low level of concern for saying thank

you to lay volunteer workers, especially those with responsibilities of limited visibility. (5)

15. The minister now sees his or her career as almost completely in the past rather than in the future. (8)

16. The congregation is convinced that if they can find a "superpreacher" to replace the departing minister, "all of our problems will be behind us." (10)

17. The leaders are unusually critical about what is or is not happening. (7)

18. One aggressive, domineering, and intimidating lay leader is allowed to exert a disproportionately large amount of power within the congregation. (8)

19. The governing body of the congregation (session, board, vestry, consistory, council) tends to see its primary role as a permission-withholding body set apart to tell the members, groups, classes, and other organizations what they cannot do. (By contrast, in the active church the governing body tends to see its role as encouraging creativity, a prophetic imagination, innovation, and whenever possible, giving permission rather than withholding it.) (7)

20. Spontaneous suggestions from enthusiastic new members tend to be ignored. (7)

21. Many of the members feel there is a perpetual financial crisis. (4)

22. New members find it difficult to gain a sense of belonging and to feel needed. (5)

23. There is a general lack of enthusiasm for outreach and mission. (6)

24. There is a high level of competence in developing arguments why "That won't work here." (9)

25. The emphasis in the teaching ministry is on learning content, not on experiences or events. (7)

26. Congregational victories, such as doubling the level of member contributions, renovating an old building, sending a mission team to work in a mission project in some other part of the world, expanding the program, enlarging

the evangelistic outreach, or purchasing a new organ are not celebrated and sometimes not even acknowledged. (8)

27. There is a great ability and a widespread tendency to turn victories into defeats. (Significant accomplishments are evaluated as "Pretty good, but not as good as what we did back in 1958" or "I was hoping it would turn out better.") (9)

28. There are limited opportunities for people to express their Christian commitment in ways that are satisfying and that provide meaningful growth experiences for the participants. (8)

29. Seniority and tenure tend to be more influential criteria in selecting leaders than competence, skill, or experience in other congregations. (7)

30. Less than one-tenth of the members are able to call more than fifty to sixty persons in that congregation by name. The typical member encounters a large number of familiar, but anonymous, faces whenever he or she attends a meeting or worship service that includes as many as one hundred persons. (6)

If the total score for your congregation adds up to more than 160 points, this probably means you are a member of a passive church. If that total is between 120 and 160 points, this may mean the amber light should be flashing and the psychological and spiritual slump that is both a cause and a product of passivity may be just ahead. If that total is between 55 and 120 points, this probably suggests some dangers of complacency, but the level of enthusiasm and optimism is sufficient to reverse the drift toward passivity. If you report a score of 30 to 55 points, you probably are a member of a comparatively healthy congregation, and you may be wasting your time by reading this book. If the score totals less than 30 points, one of four conditions probably applies: (a) this is a relatively new congregation; (b) the ideal "superpreacher" arrived on the scene very recently, and the congregation is still enjoying the euphoria of that honeymoon era; (c) you use a different system for describing reality and for adding numbers than is used by some of the rest of us; or (d) you just transferred your membership from a congregation that would have had a score of at least 180 on this test and, by comparison, this congregation appears to you to be a model of Christian vitality, enthusiasm, commitment, activity, ministry, outreach and service!

CHAPTER THREE

HOW DO WE REDEFINE ROLE?

If there is a universal prescription for passivity in the church it probably would be to seek a redefinition of role. While this is *not* the appropriate response for passivity in all churches, it is a useful strategy for a wide range of congregations. This can be illustrated by looking briefly at four different situations in which a redefinition of role is usually the best approach to combatting passivity in a congregation.

The Twenty-Year Syndrome

"This congregation began back in 1956 and my wife and I joined two years later," commented a layman from Bethany Church as he attempted to describe the present state of affairs in that 650-member congregation. "We met in a school for nearly three years and then moved into our first unit. About 1966 we completed the sanctuary and moved out of the fellowship hall where we had worshiped for seven years. I believe the enthusiasm was at its height during the 1960s. In 1969 we added an eight-room church school and office wing, and we finally got our last mortgage paid off in 1977. For the past several years we've been drifting without any real sense of direction. We peaked in size back in 1968 when we

71

reported 881 members. We added a second minister to the staff in 1972, but the decline continued, and we had to drop that position from the budget in 1976. Inflation has really hit us hard! Our utility bills are triple what they were a few years ago, and it's about all we can do now to stay current on our bills."

Hundreds of new missions founded back during the 1945–64 era followed a similar sequence. Gradually they grew to maturity, and as the years passed, began to drift into what can be described as a goalless state. Somewhere between year fifteen and year twenty-five of that congregation's history, the original goals were fulfilled. What had begun a couple of decades earlier as a neighborhood parish gradually lost its orientation to the neighborhood as members moved to new homes farther out, as a new generation of residents moved into the nearby houses and apartments, and as the members, many of whom now live some distance away, bring their friends to church. The pioneering venture of founding a new mission has been completed, and it gradually has become a mature congregation. The exciting project of planning and constructing a new building has been completed. That source of excitement has faded away. The pastor who was the "spark" that ignited the enthusiasm of the laity has moved to another parish. The charter members and near-charter members gradually have become "old-timers," but a new generation of workers and leaders does not automatically appear on the scene. Somewhere around year twenty in that parish's history, what once was a new, vigorous, and dynamic mission must recognize that it is now a mature congregation and define a new role for itself.

If and when that new role is defined, what is now a mature congregation will be able to formulate future-oriented operational goals for the fulfillment of that new role, and the congregation will be able to grow both spiritually and numerically. If a new role is not delineated, that church probably will begin to drift in an aimless manner and either decline in size or remain on a plateau.

The End of a Long Pastorate

"For twenty-eight years Dr. Harrison was the pastor here, and he was a very strong, forceful, and persuasive leader," explained a long-time member of Trinity Church. "His whole life was wrapped up in Trinity Church. He loved this congregation, the people all loved him, and we followed wherever he led us. When he told us what our priorities should be, everyone pitched in to do what was needed. After he retired, we had a very unhappy two years with a minister who was simply a bad match for this congregation. After he left, Reverend Fuller served here for seven years. He was a good preacher and an excellent pastor, but not a dynamic leader like Dr. Harrison. Since he left, we've had two more brief pastorates and have continued to drift. Today our worship attendance is about half what it was twenty years ago and our church school attendance is only about a fourth what it was during the 1950s."

Another very common type of passive congregation is illustrated by this account. Hundreds of congregations depended on the dynamic, inspiring, and challenging leadership of the same pastor for two, three, or four decades.

For most people in the larger community the name of that magnetic pastor was better known than the name of the congregation. Some knew it as Trinity Church, but many more knew it as "Dr. Harrison's church." The role of the church was wrapped up in the personality of the minister. He set the direction, established the priorities, picked the officers, formulated the goals, inspired the members, and led the way.

Eventually, however, that pastorate came to an end, and now that congregation has to establish its own distinctive identity, define a new role for itself in that community, and raise up a new generation of leaders. Until that happens, this congregation probably will drift in a sea of conflicting ideas and suggestions. Some of the old-timers will urge calling a new superpreacher. Many of the new members will place a stronger emphasis on program development. Those who are concerned about the dwindling numbers may call for a spiritual revival or for a strong evangelistic campaign. Most of the members, however, will rely on their years of training as interested, but largely submissive, spectators to wait passively to see what the future will bring.

The Adult Church

"For years Grace Church was known for its huge Sunday school," reflected Marie Hyde. "My father was the Sunday school superintendent here for over thirty years, and there were many, many Sundays when our attendance was over 400. My father had his own private goal of going over 500 on Rally Day, but I believe the closest we ever got to that was 498 one year. Today, however, the Sunday school averages between 50 and 60 in attendance, and a lot of people don't seem to care. One reason for the decline, of course, is that gradually we've become an older congregation. I'm fifty-one, and I'm one of the younger members here. The children grow up and move away, and we can't seem to attract the young parents of today. Some days I wonder if Grace Church will still be here twenty years from now."

These comments by Marie Hyde identify a third type of passive congregation that can benefit from a redefinition of role. This is the "ex-Sunday school" church. Back in the 1950s and 1960s it was built around a big Sunday school and a large number of young families. All of the lucky members of that era are now mature adults. Some have moved away, but a large core remain to reminisce about the good old days when there were two, three, or four hundred children in the Sunday school. The Sunday school church of yesterday has become the adult church of today.

HOW DO WE REDEFINE ROLE?

While there continues to be a very strong desire to attract young families, the homogeneous unit principle means that most of the new adult members are drawn from the same generation as the old-timers. What once was a strong family-oriented church has reluctantly become an adult congregation.

While very few of the members have thought about this internal inconsistency, most of the day-to-day decisions are made in a manner that reinforces the adult orientation. These include the priorities on the use of the rooms in the building, the Sunday morning schedule, the choice of hymns, the expectations the members place on the pastor, the priorities used in the assignment of lay volunteers, the allocation of financial resources, the age and value system of the minister, the role expected of children on Sunday morning, the organization and schedule of the women's group, the age of the policy makers, and the expectations placed on younger new members by the old-timers.

This congregation may continue to drift along with an aging membership that is declining in numbers, or it may decide to carve out a new role for itself and develop an aggressive evangelistic program that is consistent with that new role.

The Loss of Denominational Identity

For nearly sixty years Bethel Church was the only congregation of its denomination in this city of 48,000 residents. By the early 1950s Bethel had grown to the point that it was the largest congregation of its denomination in the state. The combination of the size of the new sanctuary completed in 1950, the central location in the state, the involvement of the pastor and of several lay leaders in denominational affairs, the supportive attitude of the members, and the prestige of the congregation made this the logical place to hold state-wide denominational conferences and conventions. In addition, on four different occasions in the decade following World War II, a national agency of the denomination had held a national meeting at Bethel. Members of Bethel Church were leaders in state-wide programs for youth, for women, for men, and in Christian education. During these years seven young men had gone from Bethel into full-time Christian service as pastors, and two others had gone into the mission field, one in South America and one in Africa. The minister who had been the pastor at Bethel from 1934 to 1949 moved from that position to a major leadership office in the denomination.

As a result of this visibility, plus the fact that it was the only church of its denomination in the city, newcomers of that denominational family who moved to the city automatically sought out Bethel. The average attendance at worship climbed from 165 in 1927, 250 in 1937, 470 in 1947, to an all-time peak of 585 in 1958.

The 1960s brought four major changes to Bethel Church. The most visible was that the minister, who had arrived in late 1949, retired in 1966 after a seventeen-year pastorate. The second most visible was the completion of the long-awaited new education building in 1965. The most gradual change was in the neighborhood surrounding the meeting place. While Bethel had not been a geographical parish since before the Great Depression, the membership had always included a substantial number of families who lived within walking distance of the building. A review of the membership roster in 1970, however, revealed that only 39 of the 641 resident members lived within one mile of the building—and 34 of those 39 were past fifty-five years of age. What had once been an upper-middle and middle-class neighborhood now was a lower-middle-class area of the city.

The most subtle, and perhaps the most devastating, change of the decade, however, came as a result of the merger. The small denomination of which Bethel had been a member united with a larger denomination to form a new denomination. This change, from being the only congregation of its denomination in the city and one of three in the county, to being the second largest of the five churches of the new denomination in the city and one of nineteen in the county, wiped out a basic part of Bethel's distinctive identity.

The minister who had arrived in 1966 remained for slightly less than three years. When he left Bethel Church, he also surrendered his ministerial credentials and is now selling insurance. The young successor, who arrived in 1969, left both his wife and family and the ministry in 1974 and has not been heard from since. He was followed by an intentional interim pastor for one year and by an elderly minister who retired in 1979 after an uneventful pastorate of four years.

The current pastor is serving a congregation that had defined its identity in (a) the denominational affiliation and (b) the leadership of two outstanding ministers who served that congregation for the period from 1934 to 1966. It, too, will drift until a new identity and role have been defined.

Role Before Goal

These four examples illustrate four types of passive churches. Each one needs to concentrate on redefining its role. These four examples also illustrate another fundamental concept in planning and goal-setting. *The definition of role takes precedence over goals!*

In one of the most influential books to be published in the past quarter century, William Glasser made three statements that have a remarkable degree of relevance to the leaders of this type of congregation.

I found that people needed involvement as a prerequisite to change . . . involvement (is) also a prerequisite to a successful role or identity . . . . The change from a survival or goal society to a successful role society is here . . . . The institutions of our society still operate as if goal took precedence over role.[1]

When translated into operational terms for the passive church, Glasser's comments offer three bits of wisdom for this effort to redefine role.

First, the wider the base of involvement of the members in this process of redefinition of role, the greater the probability that the people will accept and affirm the transition. The price tags on this broad-based involvement include (a) time, (b) patience, (c) a high level of competence by those in charge of that process, and (d) a serious and thorough educational effort to help the members understand contemporary reality. (For example, it is very difficult for many leaders of the 1960s to understand why that "new" three-story educational wing completed in 1967 is now functionally obsolete in many respects. In most states, due to recent changes in the standards for places of public assemblage, the basement rooms and the classrooms on the second floor no longer can be used for weekday programming for preschool children. "Why should we talk about building more classrooms when all of those rooms are almost like new and rarely used?" is an expression of the frustration created by the changing realities of the world.)

In congregations with over three or four hundred members it may not be possible to secure meaningful involvement in this process from more than one-fifth to one-half of the members. The trade-off becomes one of the pressures of time versus broadening the base of participation.

The second point that stands out in Glasser's observations is that in the middle of the twentieth century our culture changed from one that emphasized survival goals to one that emphasizes identity and role. For centuries the number-one question was "How do I survive?" Since 1950, according to Glasser, the culture increasingly has emphasized the issues of identity and role. "Who am I?" is now the number-one question for an increasingly large number of people.

Many of the new missions founded in the two decades following the conclusion of World War II were organized around survival goals—rallying enough members to create a new, self-supporting congregation, constructing a meeting place to house that congregation, paying off a mortgage, hiring a secretary to take part of the workload off the weary pastor, and coping with the threat of inflation.

After a couple of decades of fighting and winning the battle of survival goals, what was once a new mission now has to redefine its distinctive identity and role as a mature church. That requires a huge change in the frame of reference used to conceptualize the issues before the congregation!

A parallel can be drawn from the experiences of the congregation that knew its survival was guaranteed as long as Dr. Harrison continued as the pastor—but now Dr. Harrison is gone and with his departure the distinctive identity of that congregation has disappeared.

A similar sequence occurred at Grace Church, which had built its identity around the Sunday school, and at Bethel Church, which had found its identity in being the only church in its city from a particular denominational family. The former basis for survival and service has now been replaced by a search for identity and role. That requires a new approach to planning for ministry.

This struggle for a new identity and role also can be seen in old First Church, downtown, which for decades had built its reputation and community image on the fact that most of the community leaders and wealthy citizens of the city were members there. Nearly all those members have died, and their successors now go to one of the new and prosperous large suburban churches.[2] That change in the constituency also requires a redefinition of role.

The same size problem confronts the congregation that for years benefitted from its unique building and location as a reinforcement of its identity in the community. When the congregation voted, in what many perceived as a survival decision, to leave the historic building on that beautiful site across the street from the square that marked the center of town, the members also were voting to leave behind a part of their unique identity as a church and their role in the community.

In each of these examples, many of the members will be concerned about the survival of their congregation in the years ahead. That is not a productive approach! In the last third of this century these and similar congregations must shift their focus from institutional survival goals to a concern about identity, role, ministry, and outreach.

The third, and for this discussion, the most significant bit of wisdom to be gleaned from Glasser's comments is that role now takes precedence over goals. What does that mean?

In simple pragmatic terms it means that a new role must be defined before meaningful goals can be formulated and implemented. Attempts to formulate and implement specific operational goals in the absence of an agreed upon and widely supported definition of a new role usually produce frustration, and/or division, and/or apathy.

This basic generalization can be illustrated by referring to the four examples cited earlier. Bethany Church, founded back in 1956, must first define a new role for itself, perhaps as a regional church, perhaps as a church specializing in a high quality, avowedly Christian day school, perhaps as a congregation specializing in a ministry with single adults, perhaps as a congregation with a remarkably strong ministry for families that include a teen-ager. After that new role has been defined, but only *after* a new role has been agreed on, it will be possible to formulate specific, attainable and measurable goals designed to fulfill that new role and reinforce that new identity. By now the role of "the new church of our denomination" has been assumed by another, newer congregation.

Likewise, Trinity Church would be well advised to redefine its role in the community before seeking another minister to follow this string of successors to Dr. Harrison. How can the leaders identify the characteristics and gifts they are seeking in their next minister until *after* they have agreed on a contemporary role?

Grace Church, the former "Sunday school church" that has matured into an adult-oriented congregation, also must redefine its role, identify its assets, and agree on a new direction before it will be possible to set goals that are compatible with that role. To set goals to recreate the 1950s probably will produce more feelings of frustration than meaningful results.

Similarly, Bethel Church's unique role as the only congregation of that denomination in the city was wiped out by the merger. It now must define a distinctive identity before it can begin to articulate a new set of ministry goals.

A basic axiom in church renewal is that role takes precedence over the formulation of detailed operational or programmatic goals!

How Is This Accomplished?

How will these congregations go about redefining their roles? First of all, it must be emphasized that this will not be easy! The easiest course of action is to continue to drift in that goalless state they have been in for the past several years.

Second, the experiences of congregations in which there has been a creative redefinition of role suggests that the process usually begins at one of seven initiating points. The cycle of passivity is interrupted by a response to goallessness from one or more of these seven points.

In some connectional denominational families, the regional judicatory initiates the effort to redefine the role of a congregation which has outlived an earlier role. This is especially common in Presbyterian and Lutheran circles.

Occasionally this takes the form of asking that congregation to serve as a "pilot project," by supplying additional specialized staff, or by staffing a long-range planning committee. This can be a very creative initiating point in responding to the need to redefine role *if* the leaders are willing to invite a denominational staff member to come in and assist them.

A second initiating point, and one that is very common in congregational polity churches, is for the pastor or the staff to initiate the process and sometimes unilaterally define the new role.

A third alternative is for the laity to define the new role and to seek a minister who can help them fulfill the new role. In practice this is the least common of the six alternatives identified here, and it is most likely to occur before and/or during the vacancy period following the end of one pastorate.

A fourth response, which is both very effective and also one of the most demanding on the pastor, is to engage in a systematic, broadly based, comprehensive, and carefully managed goal-setting effort. This is not easy! Setting and implementing goals in a voluntary association in which many of the members are not in agreement on purpose and priorities is very difficult. Sooner or later the process usually will bog down, because an attempt is being made to formulate goals *before* a new role has been defined. At this point the pastor leads the congregation in the effort to define a new role, and the leaders respond creatively and affirmatively because they recognize the need for this redefinition of role. This is an application of the old cliché, "You cannot teach an adult anything that person does not want to learn." Very few church members are waiting impatiently for the opportunity to work on a redefinition of role for that parish. After several months of frustration in attempting to formulate and implement operational goals in a congregation in which there is no agreement on role, identity, and purpose, there may be a new interest in the subject. At that point a productive discussion can be launched on the redefinition of role.

The fifth response arises when external circumstances force a congregation to redefine its role. Examples of this include: the construction of a highway that forces a congregation to move to a new meeting place, the denominational merger whereby a congregation that was the only one of its denomination in the city becomes one of several congregations in the new denomination created by the merger, the influx of many new residents to what had always been a rural community, the sudden unavailability of offstreet parking which a congregation had become dependent on but did not own, a radical change in the population characteristics of the residents of the neighborhood in which the meeting place is located, or the public availability of a service program, such as a weekday kindergarten, that had been the dominant element of the congregation's community image. The externally created crisis may have such clear visibility that it forces the congregation to redefine its role.

In other words, the *external* change that contributed to the obsolescence of the old role may be the stimulus that sparks the definition of a new role.

The sixth, and one of the most effective, but least common, responses by a congregation to the need to redefine its role may come as the result of a visit by several leaders to a similar type congregation in another community. The leaders go and visit this congregation. They see a living example of a congregation that has experienced a parallel life cycle, that also found itself drifting into a goalless state, but that has already defined a new role for itself and is enthusiastically responding to this new call from the Lord. They talk with members of that congregation. They see a vision of what could happen back in their home church. They talk with the leaders of this renewed congregation and find they are not so different from themselves. They catch some of that enthusiasm and go home inspired to adapt what they have seen and heard as they redefine a new role for themselves. When it happens, this is one of the healthiest approaches to the need to define a new role.

The Use of Questions in Redefining Role

A seventh alternative in this list of initiating points in redefining role is to think in terms of specialties in ministry. This approach to redefining role can be presented in the form of a series of questions.

One application of this concept is illustrated by this set of questions.

Who will be the next one hundred adults to unite with this congregation? Why will they choose this church?

Will most of the next one hundred new members be mature adults without children at home? Why would they choose this church?

Will most of the next one hundred new members be adults who are seeking a "liberal, non-credal" church? If so, what will attract them to this congregation?

Will most of the next one hundred new members be young parents who are seeking a high quality package of programs and ministries designed to serve persons representing several generations? If so, why would they pick this parish?

Will most of the next one hundred adult new members be residents of the nearby apartments? If so, why would they choose this church?

Will most of the next one hundred adult new members be young couples expecting their first child? If so, what would attract them to this church?

Will most of the next one hundred adults who join this congregation be parents of teen-agers? If so, why would they choose this congregation?

Will most of the next one hundred new members be from families that include a handicapped member? If so, what will attract them to this church?

Will most of the next one hundred new members be recently divorced adults? If so, what will attract them to this congregation?

Will most of that next one hundred new members be persons seeking a strong Bible teaching program? If so, what will attract them to this church?

Will most of the next hundred new adult members be persons who want to be involved in ministry to others? If so, what will attract them to this congregation?

Will most of the next one hundred new members be charismatic Christians? If so, what will attract them to this congregation?

Will most of the next one hundred new members be young parents seeking a parish with a package of ministries designed for families with preschool children? If so, what will attract them to this church?

Will most of the next one hundred new members be lonely adults living alone who seek a parish that provides both a caring ministry and a challenge to their commitment? If so, what will attract them to this church?

Will most of the next one hundred new members be young single adults? If so, what will attract them to this congregation?

Will most of the next one hundred new members be "new Christians" who never before have belonged to any worshiping congregation? If so, what will attract them to this church?

Will most of the next one hundred new members be persons who are seeking a racially inclusive church? If so, what will attract them to this parish?

Will most of the next one hundred new members be persons who are seeking a church that will help them grow on their own individual spiritual pilgrimage? If so, what will attract them to this congregation?

Will most of the next one hundred new adult members be persons who have just experienced a personal or family tragedy? If so, what will attract them to this church?

Will most of the next one hundred new adult members be newcomers to this community who went church-shopping and liked what they found here? If so, what is our response to church-shoppers?

The use of these and similar questions in redefining role has several positive values.

1. These questions are designed to sharpen the evangelistic thrust of the congregation and thus reduce the chances of an excessive emphasis on institutional maintenance.

2. These questions will tend to cause the leaders to reexamine the identity and community image of the congregation, rather than focus on real estate and finances.

3. These questions will tend to cause the leaders to think in terms of the unmet needs of people outside any worshiping congregation and to design a new role in response to the needs of people, rather than in terms of an attempt to perpetuate the past.

4. These questions will tend to cause the leaders to see the necessity of making choices, rather than attempting to develop the dozens of specialized ministries required to serve everyone.

5. These questions will tend to help the leaders see that there are many choices open to that congregation as it begins to redefine its role.

6. These questions will tend to encourage the leaders to identify and affirm congregational assets and resources in redefining the role of that parish and in developing new ministries, rather than to concentrate on weaknesses.

Role and Goals Versus Passivity

After a new role has been defined, the goal-setting process usually proceeds relatively smoothly, *if* the goals are specific, attainable, and measurable, *if* the goals are consistent with the strengths and resources of that parish, *if* the goals are articulated in response to the needs of people rather than the demands of the institution, and *if* the goals are compatible with that new role. Goals are set. Resources are mobilized. New ministries are launched and the congregation is well on its way into a new era in its history.

It is difficult to overstate the value of specific, attainable, measurable, visible, and satisfying goals in combatting passivity in a congregation! Goals produce enthusiasm, open doors for people to express their commitment, encourage the emergence of new leaders, reinforce the sense of progress, encourage better stewardship, undergird the evangelistic outreach of a congregation, provide satisfactions for the members, enhance the visibility of the church, strengthen the identity of a congregation, reinforce a future orientation, and increase church attendance. But definition of role takes precedence over formulation of goals!

By contrast, unchallenged passivity in a congregation that drifts along without redefining its role and formulating new goals tends to produce lethargy, reduce the opportunities for people to express their commitment to Jesus Christ as Lord and Savior through *that* congregation, stifle giving, encourage the retention of long-time leaders who share the nostalgic recollections of the "good old days" and who are pessimistic about the future, discourage the emergence of new leaders, produce the sense of a stalemate, reinforce indecision, stifle the evangelistic outreach of the members, blur the identity of the congregation, result in an increasingly strong past-orientation, reduce the regularity of church attendance among the long-time members, suppress feelings of satisfaction, and often tends to create dissension over other minor issues.

What Is the Responsibility of the Pastor?

At this point, someone may be asking, "What is the responsibility of the pastor in helping a congregation define a new role for itself?"

Realistically, there is no simple answer to that question. The answer will depend on many variables, including (a) the distinctive characteristics of that particular parish, (b) the role of the lay leadership in that church, (c) the size of the congregation, (d) the traditions of that parish, (e) the authority and the power that are a part of the office of pastor in that denominational family, (f) the age of the members, and especially the age of the leaders when compared to the age of the minister, (g) the tenure of the pastor when compared to the tenure of the members in that congregation, (h) the community context and its impact upon that congregation's role, (i) the gifts, talents, skills, experiences, and leadership style of the pastor, (j) the number and personalities of other paid staff members, and (k) the expectations the members have of the person who holds that office of pastor.

In more general terms, however, it is possible to identify five alternative scenarios that illustrate the range of a pastor's involvement.

While it is comparatively rare, one of the best responses to this question of the pastor's responsibility was mentioned briefly earlier. This is for the congregation to define and affirm a new role for itself during a pastoral vacancy. One version of this scenario is for the congregation to be served by a full-time, or nearly full-time, intentional interim minister for six to eighteen months between what are presumed to be "permanent" pastorates.[3] The intentional interim minister can facilitate the process of redefining the role and of formulating new operational goals to fulfill that role. This effort can provide a context for an informed interview between parish leaders and the person(s) who has been identified as the probable next pastor. The definition of a new role and of the operational goals enable the leaders to articulate the gifts and special characteristics that will be needed in the next pastor.

In some regional judicatories a skilled and experienced

member of the denominational staff, rather than the interim minister, is available to serve as an outside, third-party consultant as the congregation uses the vacancy period to define a new role for itself.

This scenario offers several advantages including (a) it reduces the chances of placing the new minister in the role of "the rescuer" who is called (or sent) to rescue that goalless congregation, (b) it reduces the chances of a mismatch between the congregation and the next minister, (c) by definition of the process, it requires a strong lay role in the redefinition of role, and (d) it greatly enhances the chances that the new minister will be greeted by an active, rather than a passive, congregation.

A second scenario, and one of the most common, has been for the pastor to take the initiative and, often single-handedly, define the new role for that parish and lead the members into a new era in the history of that congregation. Hundreds of examples of this scenario can be seen in (a) most of the large, relatively new and independent or sectarian churches, especially in the South and West, (b) most downtown and inner city congregations that "have turned the corner" and reversed years of decline, and (c) most rapidly growing new missions that are built around the personality and gifts of the mission developer/pastor. This scenario is very popular among (a) lay persons born before 1935, (b) working-class churches, (c) Black churches, and (d) a small minority of white Protestant ministers.

The third scenario, and perhaps the most commendable of these five, is for the minister to function as an "enabler" and to manage the process that facilitates a broadly based participation by the members in the definition of a new role for that parish. From the pastor's perspective, this is the most demanding of the alternatives identified here. This scenario requires from the minister a tremendous quantity of energy, an unending oversight of detail, a very high degree of competence in process skills, an unreserved confidence and trust in the capabilities of the laity, an exceptional ability to conceptualize and translate abstract ideas into "picture language," the gift of being able to depersonalize tension and conflict, a leadership style that identifies and affirms strengths and potentialities and builds on those resources, a hopeful view of the future, and perhaps most significant of all, what Robert K. Greenleaf termed "a sense for the unknowable and . . . to foresee the unforeseeable."[4] While many theological seminaries have urged students to become enablers on entering the parish ministry, very few have been successful in teaching the skills and capabilities required for that role. That may be one reason why this scenario is rarely followed.

In the second scenario the pastor "does it," while in this one the minister "causes it to happen." Some of the most successful applications of a slight variation of this third scenario have been in congregations that included several influential lay leaders who were born after 1940, who have mastered many of the skills that are a part of this process, and who managed the effort on behalf of the entire congregation.

A fourth, and fairly common, scenario, builds on a distinctive characteristic, skill, gift, experience, or resource that the pastor has brought to that congregation. That gift becomes the basis for a specialized expression of ministry that becomes the first step in the redefinition of role. One congregation, for example, called a pastor who had been divorced and was happily remarried. This experience was the basis for launching a very effective ministry with divorced persons and persons in their second marriage (21 percent of all married persons are in their second or subsequent marriage).

In another church, the pastor is the mother of a Downs Syndrome child. Her experience, competence, and compassion enabled that congregation to develop a very redemptive ministry with a dozen families that included a developmentally disabled child. That specialized ministry has been the central element of a new community image for that parish.

A third example is the Presbyterian church that called a new minister who was an experienced leader of a Youth Club program. (For details of this program write Youth Club Program, Inc., 700 Dewberry Road, Monroeville, Pa. 15146.) On that foundation the congregation has built a new role as a church with an outstanding weekday program for children and youth.

In another parish this same scenario was played out when the congregation called a mature single woman as the pastor, and she helped the congregation develop a very strong ministry to young single, never-married adults in the 22 to 28 age bracket, a slice of the population that is almost completely neglected by nine out of ten congregations in every place on the continent.

Another example is the congregation that called a pastor who had a thirteen-year-old deaf child. He and his wife helped that church develop a very effective ministry for families that included a deaf member.

A more common illustration of this scenario is the congregation that builds a new identity around the radio or television ministry that features their pastor (this type of specialized ministry is very repugnant to many ministers who cannot accept the fact that all successful radio and television programs are built on the personality of an individual, not on the program offered by an institution). The Lutheran Hour, Lowell Thomas, Paul Harvey, Hour of Power, the Oral Roberts programs, and the evening network news programs on television are but a few of the many examples.

The fifth response to this question about the place of the pastor in redefining the role of a congregation is one that many ministers do find to be a very comfortable scenario. This is for the pastor to function as a teacher.

Two examples of this scenario were mentioned earlier.

The first was in the suggestion that one approach to the redefinition of role would be to go and visit congregations that have completed one chapter of their history and gone on to define a new role. For this to be an effective approach, the pastor may have to take the initiative in identifying the appropriate congregations to visit, and plan this as an educational field trip. This parallels the responsibilities of a college or seminary teacher arranging a field trip for a group of students. One essential part of that model is to choose situations that will offer a good learning experience. Another component of this pedagogical method is to be prepared to make sure the right questions are asked during the visit. A third is the debriefing or discussion following the completion of the trip and using those experiences as a part of the process of role-redefinition.

A second example of this scenario of the pastor in the role of a teacher was described earlier in that list of suggested questions that can be used to identify a potential area of specialized ministry. The pastor might begin this by using the checklist at the end of chapter 1 to help the leaders decide whether or not this is a passive congregation. The next step might be the use of the Socratic method, with the pastor asking a series of questions on resources, assets, potentialities for ministry, the central components of the heritage of that congregation, the unique traditions or the distinctive features of the denominational history, the gifts, talents, and skills of the laity of that parish, the needs of people that are not met by any congregation in that community, and the alternatives raised by the responses to these questions. By the use of the Socratic method of asking questions, the effective teacher can combine the redefinition of role and the motivation of the members to begin to write that new chapter.

Some pastors find this to be a very comfortable and productive approach to helping a congregation redefine its role.

HOW DO WE REDEFINE ROLE?

What Is the Point for Beginning This Process?

When an examination is made of the variety of roles and images projected by congregations, it turns out that most of them fall into one of five categories.

The first and most obvious of these categories is the one labeled "denominational affiliation." Many non-members as well as professionals in the churches use this system of classification to place churches in what appear to be the appropriate pigeonholes. This system is widely used whenever the discussion includes congregations affiliated with the Roman Catholic Church, the Anglican Church, The Lutheran Church—Missouri Synod, the Christian Reformed Church, the Southern Baptist Convention, the Christian Methodist Episcopal Church, the Wisconsin Evangelical Lutheran Synod, the Salvation Army, the African Methodist Episcopal Church, the Seventh-day Adventists, The Church of God in Christ, the Jehovah's Witnesses, the Church of Jesus Christ of Latter-day Saints, and several other denominational families. In each case the dominant element of the community image of a particular congregation is often that denominational label. This is especially the pattern when it is the only congregation of that denominational family in its community. As was pointed out in the first chapter, this system of classification is not especially helpful, since it tends to overlook the differences among congregations that carry the same denominational brand name.

Despite the shortcomings of this system of classification, a great many congregations attempt to define their role and their place in the community primarily by their denominational affiliation. This can be an effective approach if (a) this is the only congregation of that denomination in this community and (b) the denomination still displays strong sectarian characteristics. For congregations related to such pluralistic religious bodies, however, such as the United

93

Presbyterian Church, The United Methodist Church, the United Church of Canada, the United Church of Christ, the Christian Church (Disciples of Christ), the American Baptist Churches, the Lutheran Church in America, and the Church of the Brethren, the use of the denominational affiliation is of limited value in the redefinition of role.

A second, and also widely used, response to the question of role and community identity is to build these around the personality and gifts of a long-tenure pastor. One of the reasons why this approach is so widely used is that most people find it easier to conceptualize an institution or a movement in terms of a personality, rather than in terms of an abstract concept. This basic generalization has been illustrated by Julius Caesar, Martin Luther, William Penn, John Wesley, Roger Williams, Adolph Hitler, Norman Thomas, Franklin D. Roosevelt, Martin Luther King, Jr., Oral Roberts, Bill Gothard, Jerry Falwell, Robert Schuller, and hundreds of other leaders. The Southern Baptist Convention utilizes this basic concept by identifying their two big special missions appeals with Lottie Moon and Annie Armstrong, two famous Baptist missionaries.

One of the major objections, of course, to building the identity, role, and community image around the pastor is that, sooner or later, that minister will leave. When that pastor dies, retires, resigns, or is dismissed, the congregation must build a new image and role.

A third focal point that is used for depicting a congregation's community image is the unique design of the meeting place. The medieval cathedral is the classic illustration of this. During the 1950s this approach to defining role was expressed in the thousands of new Protestant church buildings that were designed around the three functions of worship, education, and fellowship. The huge structure housing the Sunday school or the Christian day school is a contemporary American counterpart of the European cathedral.

HOW DO WE REDEFINE ROLE?

The shortcomings that accompany this approach to projecting the identity or community image are many. They include the inflexibility of that completed building, the difficulty of expressing all the subtleties of role in a physical structure, and the simple fact of life that roles may change more frequently than the congregation is able or willing to remodel or replace that building.

A better beginning point for a discussion on role and community image can be found in the question, "Who are the people God is calling this congregation to reach and serve?" That is one of the very best beginning points for engaging in the process of redefining role and projecting a distinct identity out into the larger community. This question could be expanded to, "Who are the people who are largely overlooked or ignored by the other churches in this community whom God is calling us to reach with the good news?" The answer may produce a long list of possibilities, since in most communities one-half to two-thirds of the adult population are not actively involved in the life of any worshiping congregation.

When this approach is followed, a visitor to the community hears statements similar to these. "Oh, that is the church with the special ministry for developmentally disabled children." "That is a Korean Presbyterian church." "That is the congregation with so many young single adults." "That is the church that has resettled several refugee families." "That is a working-class church." "That is the only charismatic congregation in this community." "That is the church with so many widows." It is easy to proof-text the validity of a community identity and role reflected by statements such as these.

Finally, many congregations define and communicate their role in terms of clearly stated and precisely defined programs and ministries. For most congregations the best approach, both to a redefinition of role and a sharpening of the community image, is the combination of people and

95

programs. Who are the people your congregation is seeking to reach, and what are the programs and ministries you offer to implement this goal?

The use of that question has produced answers such as these. "We are seeking to reach that fraction of young parents who are interested in a high quality and avowedly Christian weekday nursery school based on sound principles of early childhood development." "We are reaching a number of lonely older women, most of them widowed, through our Tuesday Bible study, prayer, mutual-support, fellowship, quilting service group." "We have built one very important part of our program for high school students around a handbell choir." "Our Thursday evening group is designed to meet the needs of single adults in the 40 to 55 age bracket who are lonely." "We have a very well-organized program of adult Sunday school classes, and that is the central feature of our church. We are trying to reach adults who want to be part of a strong Sunday school." "The distinctive role of this congregation is that a number of our members have made world hunger the central concern of all facets of our program for the 1980s." "We have attempted to reach people who are interested in good Christian music, and we offer chances for participation through nine different choirs." "We are the only mainline Protestant church in town in which charismatic Christians can feel a sense of acceptance and of being needed." "We are the only church on this side of the city for folks who want to be part of a racially inclusive congregation." "We are the church for people who are actively concerned about reforming the criminal justice system." "We are the only church in town where divorced people can gain a sense of belonging and being loved. Nearly one-third of our adult members are currently divorced, and nine out of ten of them joined either by profession of faith or by reaffirmation of faith."

These are the five points for beginning this process of redefinition of role. Do you want to define your role and communicate your distinctive identity as a congregation to the larger community through your denominational affiliation? Or through the personality and distinctive gifts of you minister? Or through the design and appearance of your meeting place? Or through the people you reach, serve, and count as members? Or through distinctive programs and ministries?

Some readers will respond, "But all of these are important! How can you limit it to only one? All five factors are a part of how we define our role and of who we are as a congregation. Do you expect us to limit it to one of these?"

The answer to that question is a simple no. All five of these elements are a part of your total corporate identity, but which one do you want to reinforce and strengthen? Which one do you want to use as the beginning point in redefining your role as a congregation for the years ahead?

Five Difficult Questions

Securing agreement on a new role and creating a new community image or identity are not easy assignments! Five questions arise repeatedly as congregations become involved in this process, and a review of these may help some learn from the experiences of others.

1. "Does this mean we drop everything we have been doing and concentrate solely on this new role or on one specialty in ministry?"

That question represents an excessively simplistic view of the world and also greatly underestimates the resources and potential of most congregations. The best response to that question is, "Both/and." Continue what you are doing in terms of worship, education, nurture, missions, evangelism, witness, and other ministries and focus on the unmet needs of one slice of the population and how you might expand your total program to reach some of these people.

2. "Are you suggesting we ignore our weaknesses and

build on our strengths? Our Sunday school for children is down to less than a dozen. Shouldn't we begin by trying to rebuild that?"

The first sentence of this question earns an affirmative response. Identify and build on strengths as you define a new role! Later, after you have broken the cycle of passivity and have gained momentum, you will be better equipped to tackle some of the areas of weakness. The passive church should begin to build on strengths, assets, resources, and unique talents in defining a new role.

3. "We've been concentrating on how we can rebuild this congregation to be what it was years ago. Are you suggesting we stop trying to recreate the past?"

Yes! Jesus warned against trying to put new wine into old wineskins. Plan on new wineskins, new programs, and new approaches to ministry as you define a new role for a new era in your congregation's history.

One example of the new wineskins concept is the value of creating new classes, new groups, new choirs, new circles, and new organizations to help new members gain a sense of belonging. Do not try to channel all your new members into the long-established groups, classes, and organizations. Most people would prefer to help pioneer a new venture than to feel like aliens trying to join a long-established group.

4. "Our members are growing older. We have to reach more young people or our church will die. What do you say to that?"

That is a widespread feeling among many older leaders in thousands of congregations today. It is a natural reaction as we look around and see all our friends beginning to show their age.

A better approach, however, is not to think of how we can perpetuate this congregation, but to ask, "Who are the people out there who are not being reached and served by other churches in this community whom we have the resources and potential to reach and serve?" Jesus warned us that he who seeks to save his own life will lose it. That may apply to our efforts to save this congregation!

5. "Many of us are convinced that if only we can find the right minister for this congregation, everything will come out all right. What do you think of that?"

There is no question that pastoral leadership is very important. This book, however, is about passive churches, and one of the ways to create or to perpetuate a passive congregation is to leave everything to the minister.

You are more likely to find the "right" minister for your congregation if you redefine your role and begin to formulate some outreach goals in programmatic terms. That is the most effective beginning point for identifying the appropriate talents, gifts, and characteristics in your next minister.

CHAPTER FOUR

WHAT ARE THE ALTERNATIVES?

"That may be an interesting discussion for some people about why it is important for some types of passive congregations to redefine their role," complained a thirty-year-old layman as he participated in a workshop in church planning, "but that doesn't fit our situation. Earlier today we talked about the need to design the prescription to fit the source of the illness. What other responses, besides the redefinition of role, are open to us as we try to deal with problems of apathy and passivity?"

This is an important question, and it underscores one of the central theses of this book. The response to passivity should be tailored to the source or cause of that condition. While the redefinition of role is the appropriate response in many churches, this approach does not fit all situations. This point can be illustrated by reviewing a dozen other ways of dealing with passivity.

Apathy, Indifference, and Low Self-Esteem

There are thousands of congregations across the continent in which the leaders complain about the general indifference of the members, the excessive emphasis on institutional maintenance, and the widespread apathy. Another characteristic of most of these congregations is a low level of self-esteem. The members see this congregation as weak and having very limited potential. Most of the members have strong convictions about what cannot be done, what will not work, and what cannot be supported.

The best and the most effective response to this form of passivity is to challenge that congregation to become actively involved in a mission project outside the United States or Canada.

After hearing a missionary couple give a seven-minute presentation on the needs of people in Haiti, the members of a 213-member rural church in Ohio rallied to help support a work mission. Several months later, after hearing the first-hand reports from those who had participated in that experience, 10 percent of the members volunteered to spend two weeks of their time in Haiti to construct a badly needed community building, to staff a health clinic, and to conduct evangelistic services. The preparation for this venture, rallying the necessary support, the trip itself, the experiences of the twenty adults who made the trip, the celebration to welcome these missionaries back home on their return, and the sense of accomplishment transformed this congregation. In less than two years it changed from a church that was not able to meet its financial responsibilities to the denomination, that could "afford" only a part-time pastor, and that knew what it could not do; into an active, missions-minded, enthusiastic, and committed band of Christians who know there is no ceiling on what God can do.

One of the most effective cures for passivity is to enlist 5 to 10 percent of the adults in a venture that will involve them in an expression of their faith with other Christians in some other part of the world.

Institutional Maintenance

A parallel source of passivity in the church is an excessive emphasis on maintaining the institution. Signs of this include (a) selecting the most gifted and talented lay leaders for such responsibilities as being trustees, on the finance committee, or the personnel committee, and filling the program committee positions with the left-over members, (b) placing a high priority on rebuilding the Sunday school, not because of a desire to serve children, but primarily because the Sunday school is seen as the primary source of future members, (c) giving a higher priority to the allocation of funds for maintenance of the real estate than to missions and benevolences, and (d) adding staff to serve the members rather than to expand the outreach of the church.

What are really means-to-an-end issues become controlling factors in setting priorities and in making decisions. The building that was constructed as a house of worship becomes the master and demands the top priority in the allocation of resources. The budget, rather than a ministry agenda, becomes the place where the priorities are expressed. Instead of simply serving as a prologue for the future, the past becomes a set of sacred precedents of "how we have always done things here." All too often the tools necessary for ministry in today's world subvert the goals of the church.

The first, simplest response to this issue of an excessive emphasis on institutional maintenance is that we all have to live with what we create. After a congregation has constructed a new building, for example, it must be responsible for the utilities, the insurance, the maintenance, and the operation of that structure.

When the British House of Commons was destroyed by a German bombing attack in 1943, Winston Churchill declared, "We shape our buildings, and afterward our buildings shape us." He was arguing against the popular semicircular assembly, which allows every individual and group to move around the center, and in support of an oblong structure in which the act of crossing from one side of the aisle to the other would require serious deliberation by anyone contemplating a change in his party loyalties. In addition, Churchill argued against a new meeting place that would be large enough to seat every member of the House of Commons. He strongly preferred a small room that would facilitate easy interruptions and informal interchange and which, by virtue of being seriously overcrowded when major issues were being debated, would reinforce the sense of importance and urgency of these issues.

Every generation sets its own goals, and frequently these goals are shaped by existing buildings or result in the decision to build, remodel, or rebuild. We live with what we create. When a congregation creates a powerful board of trustees by selecting the most influential members of that parish to serve as trustees, it must live with the results of that action. Or, when a congregation selects the most influential leaders of that church to serve on the finance committee, it must live with the consequences of that decision.

A second response to the issue raised here is to change the sequence in selecting lay volunteers for policy-making positions in the church. Before the nominating committee meets, the basic policy-making body of that congregation (session, council, board, vestry, consistory, etc.) should meet and respond to this question, As we try to understand and respond to what God is calling this congregation to be and to do, what is the most important concern on our agenda for the coming year?

If that governing body decides the most important concern for the coming year is evangelism, it could instruct the nominating committee to make, as its top priority, the selection of the most competent, gifted, and committed members available to serve on the evangelism committee. This should be done before anyone is nominated for any other office or committee.

If the governing board concludes that the top priority for the coming year should be Christian education, it would instruct the nominating committee to seek to place the most talented, influential, and dedicated members available to serve as teachers and/or on the education committee before making any other nomination.

If that governing body should decide that world peace (Matthew 5:9) is the most urgent item on the churches' agenda today, a recommendation will be forthcoming that persons who hold that view, and who also are influential leaders in that congregation, will be asked to devote most or all of their efforts as lay volunteers to the work of a committee seeking to promote world peace.

Some readers will recognize this procedure as contrary to that followed in many congregations where the nominating committee first fills the administrative offices (president of the congregation, treasurer, trustees, finance committee, governing board, etc.) and then fills the vacancies on the program committees (worship, education, evangelism, social action, etc.) from the list of members not already chosen for administrative offices.

The procedure suggested here is based on four assumptions. First, it is assumed that in most congregations the pastor and/or a relatively small number of lay leaders have a disproportionately large amount of influence in determining direction, defining purpose, and setting priorities.

Second, it is assumed that any office or committee post influences the holder of that position to look at the world from the perspective of that office or committee. In other words, the "behavior setting" or office influences the perspective, behavior, values, and priorities of the person holding that office. The longer the person remains in that behavior setting or office, the more that person's perspective is shaped by that office.

Third, it is assumed that the operational definition of purpose is not controlled by a generalized statement adopted as a part of the charter or at a congregational meeting, but is defined by the values, priorities and experiences of that small group of very influential leaders. If the most influential members serve as trustees, they will tend to make care of the real estate the top priority for that congregation. If the six or seven most influential members serve on the Christian education committee, they will tend to make education the top priority in that parish.

Thus if the most influential leaders are asked to serve on the finance committee for several years, it should not be surprising to find that church finances have become the most important concern of that church.

Fourth, it is assumed that every Christian congregation should be *intentional* about its purpose, role, goals, direction, ministry, and program. Therefore, in response to those who ask, "But doesn't this procedure boil down to a rather blatant manipulation of the nominating committee?" the answer is "Yes!" If the word "manipulate" is defined in neutral terms as "an intentional effort to influence the values, direction, and behavior patterns of individuals and institutions," then this is an intentional effort to influence the behavior pattern of a congregation, so that the primary reasons for its existence and its basic purpose are given the highest priority in the assignment of lay volunteers.

In other words, the priorities used in assigning influential lay volunteers to offices, committees, and boards may be the most influential single factor in determining the purpose and operational priorities of many congregations! Therefore, these assignments should be made in a manner that is consistent with the values and goals of that congregation.

An alternative response concerns the concept of rotation in office. In general, the longer an influential lay leader holds a particular office or serves on one committee, the more confortable that person feels in that position and the more likely that person will be increasingly convinced of the importance of that particular committee's work and responsibilities. A fairly common example is the board of trustees that has had the same membership for several years. As the years pass, that board becomes increasingly influential in the life of that congregation, and real estate becomes a very high priority. A few congregations have responded to this pattern by limiting a person's membership to one three-year term on the trustees, finance committee, and governing board, but have not imposed any limit on how long one person may serve on such committees as missions, planning, education, world peace, social concerns, evangelism, worship, or community outreach.

The rotation-in-office concept is used to minimize the influence of the boards and committees focused on institutional maintenance and on means-to-an-end concerns, while longer tenure is encouraged for persons serving on committees charged with planning and implementing the ministry goals of that congregation.

In summary a congregation can build passivity into program development and create activity in institutional maintenance by the priorities used to guide the nominating committee. What are the priorities in the nominating process in your congregation?

Staff-Centered Ministries

What is the appropriate response when nearly all the programs the members hold in high esteem are largely "owned and operated" by the paid staff? Examples of this may include the music program, youth ministries, Christian education, parish calling, preaching, and hospital visitation. When members point to staff-centered programs as the strongest components of congregational life, this may be a sign of passivity.

If it is, the best response is to focus on developing more ministries and programs "owned and operated" by the laity. The most common example of this type of program in many denominations is the women's organization. That may serve as a model for the next steps. Other examples of lay-controlled programming often include the adult Sunday school classes, a men's organization, the completely volunteer choir, the food cooperative, the weekly visitation to residents of a nearby nursing home, care of the bereaved following the death of a family member, Bible study groups, prayer chains, and the resettlement of refugee families.

Following the Authoritarian Pastor

Sometimes the departure of the highly directive and long-tenured pastor means the congregation must redefine its role. In other situations, however, it may mean retraining the lay leadership for a new and more aggressive role.[1] When the lay leadership of a parish has been trained for a decade or two to passively follow the minister's instructions, it is unreasonable to expect that they automatically will assume a more active role immediately after the arrival of a new pastor. Some newly arrived successors seek to combat this form of passivity by combining the retraining of some of the long-time leaders with the infusion of several new activist leaders.

The Strong Past-Orientation

One of the many sources of passivity in congregations is an excessively strong past-orientation. When that is the diagnosis, the obvious response is to build in a strong future-orientation.

A creatively redundant system for strengthening the future-orientation of a congregation might include (a) changing to a multi-year approach to budgeting by adding a couple of vertical columns to the right-hand side of the budget preparation worksheets to include estimates for the year after next and the year after that, (b) adopting a systematic process for setting goals for the coming year, (c) adding a "peek into the future" to the end of the annual celebration of the church's anniversary, (d) scheduling an annual solicitation from the members of ideas about what they would like the future to bring to this congregation, and (e) redesigning the annual officers' planning retreat to include a strong future-orientation structured into the schedule.

One of the most effective means of building a stronger future-orientation into a congregation is through an expansion of the reporting system at the annual meeting. *In addition* to asking each program committee and organization to report on what it did during the past year, ask each one to include in its annual report responses to questions such as these:

(1) What do you plan to do during the coming year? What are your objectives?

(2) How do these objectives relate to the overall purpose of this church?

(3) What, in specific terms, are the programs you plan to use to achieve these objectives?

(4) What will be the resources you will need to implement these programs during the coming year? Which of these resources, including lay volunteers, have been committed to these programs?

(5) How do you plan to evaluate the effectiveness of these programs?

Another congregation combines the celebration of events in the lives of the members with a visual reminder that God has promised us a tomorrow. The nature of that system was described by a member to a visitor.

"We have a large banner hanging in the sanctuary at Trinity," explained Mrs. Anderson, a member of this nineteen-year-old suburban congregation. "Whenever there is a birth, a death, a wedding, a graduation from college, or some other major event in the life of a member of our congregation, that event is recognized the following Sunday. During the worship hour an appropriate symbol commemorating that event is pinned to the banner. Sometime during the following few days a member of the Dorcas Circle will come over and sew these to the banner so they don't get lost. Last Sunday, for example, three symbols were pinned to the banner. Roland and Marie Carter and their three children are moving to Houston, so Marie had cut out of a piece of red felt a picture of a van—everyone here knows they drive a red Ford van—and sewed the word "Carter" on it. During the announcement period when the minister noted that this was the Carter's last Sunday here, the five of them went over and pinned this little red piece of felt on the banner. Following this, the minister announced that on Friday an 8½-pound baby boy had been born to Ken and Becky Garner. As the proud father went over to pin a baseball, a circle of white felt with the baby's name on it, to the banner, our congregation burst into applause. The Garners have been married for six years, and this is their first child. Next the minister announced that this Saturday, Helen Gerlach will be receiving her master's degree. Helen is a grandmother now and went back to school when her youngest child was in high school. Three or four years ago she received her bachelor's degree, and then she decided to go on to graduate school. When the minister announced this event, Helen went over and pinned a little cloth scroll representing a diploma on the banner."

"How do you build a future-orientation into that process?" asked the visitor.

"When we started this, of course, we only had the one banner," replid Mrs. Anderson. After three years we saw that three was about the right number for the wall in the nave, so all the older ones are hung in the corridor in the educational wing."

"Which three do you hang in the sanctuary?" was the next question.

"This year's, last year's, and the next year's," responded Mrs. Anderson. "In 1974 our minister preached a sermon on the freedom God has given each of us and how we should see our future here on earth as open-ended. In response to this sermon the Dorcas Circle immediately prepared a new banner with the date 1975 on it, and the following Sunday there were three banners on the wall. On the left was the completed banner for 1973, in the center was the banner for that year, and on the right was the blank banner for the coming year. Ever since then we have kept last year's banner on the left, the current year in the center, and a blank banner for the coming year on the right. This has turned out to be helpful in strengthening the future-orientation of our congregation. That blank banner for next year reminds them that next year is still an open book."

That's an idea our congregation could use, mused the visitor. *Our women's organization has a coed Bible study circle, and this would be a good project for them.*

Distrust of Church Finances

"I want to know what's going on here!" demanded Joe Wallis as he stormed into the office at Calvary Church one Thursday morning in January. "My wife brought home the financial report from the annual meeting Tuesday night, and it says here that our church gave only $150 last year for world hunger. When we had that special offering I personally put a check for $200 in an envelope that was clearly marked World Hunger. Are you trying to tell me the rest of the people gave minus fifty dollars?"

"That's not quite the way it works," explained the pastor. "Every year the board decides how much this congregation will give for the special offerings. In making up last year's budget the board allocated $150 to world hunger. If the special offering is less than that, we make up the difference out of the general fund. If the special offering brings in more, the excess goes into the general fund. That way every special appeal is guaranteed its budgeted amount."

"That's not how it was presented that Sunday we had the special offering!" protested Joe. "We were given to understand that whatever we gave would go to world hunger. That's why I wrote out a check for $200. I believe that is a worthy cause, and I wanted to support it. From now on, I'll give directly to the causes I believe merit support."

One of the most effective means of undermining the trust level within a congregation, of lowering morale, of increasing passivity, and of creating disharmony is to create a situation that causes members to believe they cannot trust the financial accountability system of that parish.

Obviously the best response to this source of passivity is very simple. Do not let it happen! The financial appeals, the allocation of funds, and the system of record-keeping should be internally consistent.

Once something has happened to create this distrust, the best response is full disclosure. In many churches there is complete disclosure of all expenditures, including salaries and detailed program expenses. In other congregations the leaders apparently believe the members should not know the details on benevolences, salaries, program expenses, and other expenditures. This second group of churches is trading the benefits of secrecy for the risk that erroneous or misleading information will be circulated and the confidence the members have in the financial system may be undermined. Is secrecy worth that risk?

The Mismatch

An informed guess is that in any given month perhaps 5 percent of all Protestant congregations in the United States and Canada are immobilized because the gifts, talents, experience, and skills of the current pastor do not match the needs of that congregation at this point in its history. Some denominational leaders will agree with the generalization, but argue that the proportion is closer to 10 percent.

In a few cases it might be more accurate to recognize that the minister simply is incompetent. That is a misreading of most situations, however. In one case, for example, the young associate minister, after only three years of experience beyond seminary, was called to succeed the retiring senior minister of a 2300-member congregation.

In another case, a minister, who had spent thirty years as a missionary serving a group of very small congregations in South America, returned to the United States and accepted a call to a nineteen-year-old, 800-member congregation that was experiencing the "twenty-year syndrome" and needed an experienced pastor to help it redefine its role.

In a third case, a minister, who had been serving as a very effective denominational executive for eleven years, came back into the parish ministry. During his years in a denominational office he had perfected his conceptual skills and his administrative ability—but at the cost of a sharp decrease in his competence in interpersonal relationships.

In a fourth example, a minister, who had had three very effective pastorates in small town churches, one day found his professional dream fulfilled. He was now the pastor of a city church. Unfortunately, however, it was not "just another city church." It was a relatively small and numerically declining, country-club type congregation. This pastor moved from a parish where he was near the top of the socio-educational pecking order to a congregation where he was among the least-well-educated male members and clearly at the bottom of the socio-economic pecking order. For two years this "behavior setting" immobilized him, and his inability to lead immobilized the congregation.

Dozens of examples could be cited to illustrate this term "mismatch." The question is, What can be done about it?

While there are no easy solutions to this, one of the most traumatic sources of passivity in the church, here are four generalizations that do merit consideration.

First, if at all possible, avoid "choose-up-sides" polarization tactics. In one congregation, for example, the president of the congregation called a meeting that all members were invited to attend. He announced that he would grant anyone who wanted to speak one three-minute block of time, but the speakers would be alternated between those who wanted to speak on behalf of the pastor and those who wanted to speak against the minister. Avoid that type of public hearing! Minimize the events and circumstances that will create a pastor-versus-congregation situation.

2. The most effective method of minimizing that pastor-versus-congregation impasse is for the minister and a small group of responsible lay leaders (elders, deacons, the pastoral relations committee, vestry, council, consistory, etc.) to agree on the selection of a third-party mediator. This might be a denominational staff person, the ministerial relations committee of presbytery, the bishop, the regional minister, or a complete outsider.

3. Give this outside mediator the opportunity to talk with several persons on a one-to-one basis before that first meeting with the pastor and the lay leaders. These half-hour interviews should include (a) the pastor's spouse, if interested and available, (b) the church secretary, (c) the three or four most influential and respected lay persons in the congregation, (d) the pastor, (e) other staff members, such as the associate minister, intern, director of Christian education, vicar, or choir director, and (f) the pastor of a nearby congregation who may be knowledgeable about that situation.

4. If it appears this is clearly a mismatch or genuine incompatibility between the congregation and the minister, it may be wise for the outside mediator to keep the discussion focused on how the situation can be resolved, rather than spend hours listening to speeches that have been given many times earlier. This discussion should include the steps to be taken by both parties, agreement on a time line or schedule and, if it appears appropriate, agreement on a date by which time that pastor-parish relationship will have been terminated. From this outsider's experience, in nine cases out of

ten, the passivity created by the mismatch will not be broken in a creative manner until after the forthcoming change of pastors has been announced with a precise date included in that announcement.

An alternative response, which has been widely used during the past century, but is not recommended here, is for the pastor and his supporters to form a new congregation while the opponents also form what in effect is a new congregation. Sometimes congregations have had some very lively battles over title to various assets, but that is not the best way to combat passivity in a church!

The Premature Announcement of Retirement

A closely related source of passivity may be the minister's announcement, two or three years ahead of time, of the date of retirement. This is most likely to immobilize the congregation if (a) this has been a long pastorate and the congregation and pastor gradually have grown apart, (b) there has been a growing bloc of opposition to the pastor and this announcement is perceived as an effort to "buy time," (c) if it is a multiple staff church with obvious disharmony among the staff and this announcement is perceived as an effort to force the early resignation of another staff member, and/or (d) the stated date repeatedly is postponed to a later time.

The best response to this source of passivity is to avoid it. A few denominations have a tradition that retirement dates cannot be announced more than twelve months in advance. Occasionally the letter of call contains a provision that will prevent this trap.

In dozens of congregations the frustrated leaders have arranged to "buy up the pastor's contract" and pay the minister a lump sum to move up the retirement date.

A third response is to adopt the procedure suggested in the

previous section and bring in an outside mediator to help negotiate an agreement to end the impasse.

The Veto Board

It is not unusual for a recently arrived minister to discover that the greatest competence of the governing board is to explain why any suggested innovation "will not work here" and therefore has to be disapproved. In many churches the board has been practicing this skill for many years, and like every one of us who has a special competence, enjoys doing what it has learned to do so well.

One response to this source of passivity is to help the board distinguish among three different types of actions. When the board approves one category of proposals, that action carries with it not only approval, but also support. For example, the decision to approve a recommendation to replace the roof carries with it the responsibility for financial support. A second category of decisions involves not only disapproval, but a prohibition on anyone's going ahead despite the board's disapproval. Between those two extremes on the decision-making spectrum is a wide area where the board is involved in permission-giving or permission-withholding *without* necessarily either approving or disapproving.

For example, the board might be divided on a proposal to change to two Sunday morning worship services, beginning with the second Sunday in September. Instead of seeking a majority vote to approve, or to disapprove that change, it might be wiser to explain this is an issue that belongs in the permission-giving middle of that decision-making spectrum. The board members are not committing themselves to attend both services, or even to worship at the "new" hour. All that is being sought is permission to add one more opportunity on Sunday morning for people to gather for the corporate worship of God. The real "vote" of approval or disapproval will come from the people who attend, or stay away from, that new service.

If the board that has been inclined to reject all new ideas can comprehend the existence of this middle section of the decision-making spectrum, they may be able to develop a new competence in permission-giving that is not necessarily the same as approval.[2]

A second approach to this source of passivity is to give the board more practice in approving new ideas. After they have gained more experience in being "for" than being "against," they will find it easier to drop that automatic veto posture.

One way of accomplishing this is to adopt a policy that every new idea must be either referred to the appropriate committee or held over for the next board meeting before any action can be taken. In general, most people are inclined to reject any new idea when it is first presented. Giving the board members more time to consider the new idea increases the chances that the board will be more open to it.

A second part of this approach is to introduce fewer proposals that call for major or multiple changes and concentrate on changes by addition. The addition of a second worship service to the Sunday morning schedule can be used to illustrate this point. One approach would be to introduce a complex proposal that includes both the addition of a second service and changing the time for Sunday school and the other worship service. That provides a variety of points for opposition. Some members may favor the addition of a second worship experience, but oppose the new Sunday school schedule. A better and less disruptive approach would be to leave the rest of the schedule untouched and simply add another worship experience, either early or late on Sunday morning.

A third part of this approach is to solicit new program suggestions from board members and to involve them in the generation of the proposals the board has to approve or disapprove. A common method of implementing this concept is to have every board member serve on one or more of the committees that originate the proposals that subsequently come before the board.

Inadequate Internal Communication

"You really have to be on the board to know what's going on around here," explained a long-time member of Hillcrest Church. "When I was on the board I knew everything, but now I'm pretty much in the dark. I guess that explains why I'm not as active as I used to be. It's hard to stay interested if you don't know what's going on."

Many congregations, and the vast majority of those with more than three hundred members, encourage passivity among the members by maintaining an inadequate internal communication system. In a few churches the situation is made even worse by the repeated declaration, "It's up to the members to keep themselves informed." What may be equally devastating is the rejoinder, "Well, everything is in the newsletter and the bulletin. If they would read these, they would be informed."

There are four fallacies in that assumption. First, not everything is covered in those pieces of paper. Second, to place the burden for being informed on the members is a losing tactic and an abdication of leadership responsibilities. Third, to assume the printed word is an adequate channel of communication is a counterproductive assumption in this age of visual communication. Finally, the only safe assumption is to assume that the burden of communication is on the sender of the message, not on the recipient.

A better approach would be based on this set of five assumptions.

1. Activity and involvement are related to the person's knowledge of what is happening.

2. Whenever possible, use visual media (slides, films, pictures, videotapes, etc.) to communicate.

3. All *important* messages should be sent out at least on *five* different channels of communication. These channels might include (a) face-to-face oral communication, (b) telephone calls, (c) letters, (d) announcements in the bulletin, (e) pictures and announcements on the bulletin board, (f) the local newspaper, (g) the church newsletter, (h) the coffee hour, and (i) the radio.

4. The basic responsibility for, and the control over, the internal communication system in a parish rests largely with the sender of the messages, not the recipients.

5. If in doubt, be redundant, rather than economical, in communication.

In general, the larger the membership, the greater the probability that poor internal communication will enhance the passive stance of those members who are not in leadership offices.

A Congregation of Strangers

"Our problem here at Westminster Church is that the members simply do not know one another," complained a member of that 1600-member congregation. "We have two worship services every Sunday morning, and we have to receive nearly 200 members a year just to stay on a plateau."

That complaint describes a common source of passivity in larger congregations and/or in those with more than a 10 percent annual turnover in the membership. Whenever a person enters a group in which most of the people present do not know one another by name, there is a strong temptation to lapse into a passive stance. That happens every Sunday morning in thousands of Protestant churches all across the nation.

The obvious response to that condition is to encourage more members to become better acquainted with other members. Among the most widely used methods to accomplish this are (a) encouraging every member to wear a name tag, (b) providing a social time (coffee hour) following each worship service and designing the building to funnel all attenders in and through the same large room (in many buildings this can be accomplished simply by changing where the minister stands to greet people after worship), (c) the generous display of pictures of members on the bulletin board, (d) regular fellowship events that are planned around a large group, rather than a small group format, (e) the generous use of names in the church newsletter, and (f) posting large display cards on the wall in a heavily used corridor that carry both name and photograph of every officer and leader or the photograph and name of every new member or the photograph and name of every leader, teacher, and worker in every organization in that congregation.

The Multi-Church Parish

Thousands of ministers serve two or three or more congregations in what is usually described as a "yoked field," a "circuit," or a "multi-church parish." It is easy for one or more of the congregations served in these arrangements to lapse into a passive stance and simply focus on keeping the doors open. It also is unrealistic to expect the pastor to be able to break that cycle of passivity in two or three churches within the limitations of a two- or three- or four-year pastorate. What are the alternatives?

One possibility is for the pastor to concentrate all the available discretionary time on the congregation that shows the greatest promise, while carrying out only the essential responsibilities at the other church(es). This strategy may create some discontent among the people who feel neglected and who may resent what appears to them to be excessive attention on the one church.

Another approach would be to follow one of the lay-centered strategies described earlier, such as participating

119

in a work mission project in another country or initiating some new lay-dominated ministries.

A third alternative, and one that is gaining increasing support in several denominations, is to minimize the number of situations in which one pastor is asked to serve two or more congregations. This alternative is based on the assumption that having a part-time pastor who holds a secular job, but who is available to that congregation all day Sunday and on several evenings, is a more productive arrangement for the small-membership congregation that is sharing a pastor with another congregation.

The sharp increase in the number of seminary-trained persons who are available for part-time pastorates has made this a far more feasible alternative than it was a decade or two ago. This arrangement gives the pastor of the small membership church a greater opportunity to concentrate on only one congregation, but the weekday employment of the pastor reduces the temptation for the laity to become excessively dependent on the minister.

In addition to the redefinition of role, and to the dozen alternative responses described in this chapter, there is one other response to passivity that deserves serious consideration. It may be the best response to the problems facing the passive church. This response is based on the assumption that new members bring with them some unique assets—but that is another chapter.

CHAPTER FIVE

NEW MEMBERS:
ASSETS OR LIABILITIES?

"The discussion at our circle meeting the other night got around to our new minister's sermons," observed Martha White, a long-time member of Salem Church, to a close friend of many years. "You know what I think of his preaching! Half the time I can't understand what he's talking about, he's way over my head. The other half of his sermons aren't worth listening to; they sound like he's making them up as he goes along, that he hasn't prepared. What got me, however, was that three of the younger women there Tuesday night claimed he's the best preacher they've ever heard! That nearly knocked me off my chair when I heard it. I can't tell you their names, all three are new here, but I sure was surprised to hear them bragging about his preaching."

"Well, I don't care much for his sermons either," agreed her friend, "but he sure is bringing in the new members. Last Sunday there were four more couples and two single persons who came forward and took the vows of membership. If he keeps on bringing new members in at that same rate for the next year or two, this certainly will be a different church!"

"Yes, and I'm not sure I'm going to like it," replied Martha. "These new people want to change too many things too fast. The other night someone mentioned there was talk about going to two services on Sunday morning. I don't know why anyone would propose that since the only time we fill the sanctuary now is on Easter, but I suppose if enough of the new members want to change it, they'll change it."

This conversation introduces one of the most effective means of wiping out passivity in a congregation. A flood of new members is the most effective route to church renewal.

This conversation also illustrates one of the price tags on this response to passivity. The larger the flood of new members, the more innovations they introduce, the more influential they are in changing the congregational life-style from passive to active, the greater the impact the new members have on the decision-making processes, the stronger the influence of these new members in redefining the role of that congregation, and the more successful they are in developing new programs—the greater the chances some of the long-time members will feel threatened by the changes.

This conversation also introduces a widely neglected issue that should be of major interest to anyone interested in church renewal, church growth, evangelism, the assimilation of new members into a long-established congregation, or combatting passivity in the churches. It is also a subject that will be of special interest to those who recognize the value of using the median tenure of the members as a system for classifying churches (see chapter 1). In general, new members are different in many respects from long-time members, and those differences are extremely important to the passive church. Before getting into a discussion on why new adult members are distinctive assets, however, it may be helpful to identify some of the differences between new and long-term members.

How Are They Different?

The most widespread, the most subtle, and the most significant difference between the majority of new adult members and many of the long-time members is *why* they are in the congregation *today*.

Some of today's older members are still in their church, even though they have moved to a new residence, and it would be more convenient and economical to go to a church closer to their home. Other members were attracted to their congregation by a particular pastor who has since moved on, but they have remained. Some may have come because the church met the needs of their children, but the children are now grown and gone, and the parents are still there. A few came because of a particular program or ministry that is no longer offered, but they, too, are still there. Many came at the invitation of a friend, a neighbor, or a relative who has since departed; but they are active and regular members of their church. A substantial number may have been brought by their parents. The parents have either moved away or died, but the children are still in the church as adults.

To state the fact simply, the reason a substantial number of present *long-time* members originally joined the church is not the same reason they continue as members today. People join a church for a variety of reasons. But, in general, the basic reason they are still members, many years later, is that they have built up deep relationships with (a) the people in that congregation and (b) that particular sacred place. These are valid reasons for continuing to be members of that congregation for many years, but these also may be factors that feed passivity in a congregation.

By contrast, most *new* adult members join a church—and become active in that congregation—because it offers a meaningful response to their personal and spiritual needs and those of the members of their family. In general terms, a congregation meets the religious and spiritual needs of new members through functional programming (including corporate worship), while in that same congregation the religious and spiritual needs of many of the long-time

123

members are met through relationships with other long-time members and with that sacred place.

One very significant implication of this insight is that new adult members tend to have a different value system in considering proposals for change than that of long-time members!

A second difference between new and long-term members is the fact that new members from one era in a congregation's history may have been attracted to the church for different reasons than those from the present era.

A simple example is that people join a new mission because they are challenged to be a part of a pioneering venture. Fifteen years later, that challenge has lost most of its attractiveness. In one era of another congregation's history, it was the pastor who attracted new members, while in another era it may have been the Sunday school. During the 1920s, for example, many people joined Redeemer Church because they lived in that neighborhood, but today very few residents of the neighborhood are members of Redeemer. In the early 1950s Immanuel Church attracted many young couples with small children. Twenty-five years later most of the new members are empty-nest couples in their fifties.

The reason behind a person's original decision to unite with a congregation will have a significant impact on that member's response to any proposal for change!

Since new members often have different reasons for joining today's congregation than what motivated the persons who joined ten or twenty years ago, it is only logical to expect different responses to new ideas.

A third important truth is that new members tend to be more enthusiastic about the congregation than some of the old-timers who have endured one or more disillusioning experiences there. For example, it usually is the older, long-time member who declares, "I'm afraid this is a dying church." After thousands of interviews with new adult members, I have yet to hear anyone respond, "The reason I

chose this congregation is because it was a dying church."
Any *per capita* pessimism that may be extant in a local
church tends to be greater among long-time members than
among newcomers, *regardless of age!*

A fourth significant difference between most new adult
members and long-term *active* members is reflected in the
"sense of belonging." Active old-timers usually feel they
have been completely assimilated and have earned a sense of
belonging. Most new members still feel like outsiders and
have yet to acquire this sense of belonging. The old-timers
talk about "we, us, ours." The newcomers talk about "they,
them, theirs." Many of the long-time members feel that "I've
already served my term." This distinction is very important
in enlisting lay volunteers.

The longer a person lives in any particular place or setting,
the stronger the attachment to that place and to the
memories that place evokes. The older a person is, the more
memories of the past that person carries. This produces a
fifth distinction between the newcomers and the old-timers
that is especially pronounced between the younger new
members and the older long-term members. In general, the
new young adult members tend to be more future-oriented,
while the older long-term members tend to be more
past-oriented.

Perhaps the most startling generalization on this distincti-
veness of the new adult member emerged from the study,
The Unchurched American, published by The Princeton
Religion Research Center. This study contrasted "the
churched" and "the unchurched" and discovered that nearly
one-half of the churched adults were brought up in the
congregation with which they now identify themselves. By
contrast, most of the new adult members were *not* brought
up in that church.

In other words, most adult new members bring a fresh
perspective of how another congregation functioned, while

many of the long-time members do not have the benefit of that additional perspective.

As a result of these and other factors, a seventh difference is that the newcomers tend to be more open to innovation, creativity, and new ideas, while long-term members tend to be more concerned with perpetuating the status quo and protecting the institution. Martha White intuitively recognized this distinction, felt threatened by it, and feared the change of pace the newcomers might bring to Salem Church.

Of special interest to pastors is an eighth difference between newcomers and old-timers. Out of any large collection of adult new members the vast majority have strong positive feelings about the minister. Most would not have joined their congregation if they had disliked the pastor. By contrast, it is not unusual for many of the long-term members to be dissatisfied with the current minister. Frequently they compare the current minister with the person who was their pastor back when they joined. The "new minister" comes out on the short end of most such comparisons. One implication of this is that efforts to force the departure of the current minister frequently originate with, and are supported by, the old-timers, not the newcomers.

Finally, newcomers tend not to be as attached to the present location and building that is the meeting place for the congregation as are the old-timers. To the new members the building is merely a place, it is not yet a *sacred* place. One result of this is that hundreds of congregations now meeting in functionally or structurally obsolete buildings will remodel or rebuild during the 1980s because new members will initiate and support that decision. In hundreds of similar situations the congregation will continue to meet in an obsolete, perhaps poorly located, building because the older members outnumber the newcomers and successfully oppose such a decision.

Assets or Liabilities?

In addition to the differences already noted, there are a half-dozen very significant implications of these differences between the old-timers and the newcomers that are influential in combatting passivity. These implications merit the thoughtful consideration of anyone seriously interested in church renewal and in redefining the role of a parish.

The first, and by far the most important, implication centers on whether new adult members are perceived by the long-term members as threats and potential liabilities or as assets and potential resources.

Martha White felt threatened by the differences between herself and the newcomers. Many long-time members feel threatened, angered, or frustrated when new members propose remodeling or selling the meeting place, changing the Sunday morning schedule, adding new ministries, expanding the staff, or revising the program.

The destructive and counterproductive response to these differences is for the old-timers to perceive the newcomers as a liability, a problem, and (for the most part) irresponsible. The new members, as a result, see the long-time members as a collection of recalcitrant stalwarts, opponents to creativity and (for the most part) a liability. However, suggestions by the newcomers and the responses by the old-timers can be handled creatively when diagnosed as normal and predictable behavior patterns resulting from the differences between long-term members and new members.

A second productive implication is that most congregations draw a disproportionately large number of Sunday school teachers, youth counselors, and other workers from the new adult members. In part, this is a result of the newcomers' desire to be assimilated. The old-timers have already been assimilated and feel they have fulfilled their worker obligations.

This is an especially significant point in those congregations that practice "assimilation by works" (not to be confused with salvation by works!) rather than emphasizing the assimilation of newcomers in and through the group life of the parish. In many congregations, the two main avenues for the assimilation of newcomers are to join groups, classes, and circles dominated by old-timers, and to accept the jobs and tasks that the old-timers did when they were younger and are now weary of doing. In those congregations many of the old-timers, however, still are willing to be policy-makers; they have "graduated" from the "worker" category of membership. Newcomers often have to "earn" this feeling of belonging before they are eligible to be promoted to serving as policy-makers.

This should *not* suggest, however, that newcomers are eligible to be workers but should be barred from becoming policy-makers until after they have served a five-year apprenticeship. In many passive churches, however, the passivity is reinforced, and the tension between the newcomers and the old-timers is heightened, by expecting the new members to volunteer as workers, but excluding them from that inner circle of policy-makers. This informal probationary period for new members may last for three or four years, or longer, before they are deemed eligible to be policy-makers. By that time, however, many of the most creative and competent will have found other channels in the community through which they can express their creativity and commitment, or they will have moved to a new community.

The third implication is that since newcomers tend to be more future-oriented, more open to new approaches, more sensitive to what the congregation currently does best in ministry, more creative, less tied to the past, more enthusiastic about that congregation and its propects, and more in touch with what attracts new members *today*, it might be wise to have a disproportionately large number of new members in policy-making positions.

Fourth, because of their enthusiasm for what the congregation is today, their general support of the current pastor, and their future-orientation, adult new members constitute an excellent source from which to draw persons to serve on the church growth or evangelistic task force. The people who have just "bought the product" are the best people to sell it. This may help break that cycle of passivity by accelerating the rate at which new members join the fellowship.

Fifth, a general rule is that new groups attract new members. Most people prefer to be pioneers rather than Johnny-come-latelys. Therefore, rather than attempting to direct new adult members into existing classes, groups, circles, and other organizations, it is often better to encourage many of the new members to be the pioneers in creating new classes, circles, and groups. New members join the church to have their religious needs met, not to help perpetuate long-established—perhaps declining—groups of ex-pioneers! New groups of new members will attract additional new members much more effectively than long-established groups composed largely of long-time members.

In other words, new members usually constitute the best source of allies for launching new face-to-face small groups and of charter members of these new groups. One of the common characteristics of the passive congregation is that it is now seven, ten, or fifteen years since the last new face-to-face group was organized. One way to combat that, as well as to facilitate the assimilation of the new members, is to turn to new members to help create new study groups, prayer cells, Sunday school classes, or other face-to-face groups.

Finally, since new members tend to be enthusiastic and supportive of the current pastor, perhaps they should be represented in disproportionately large numbers on the pastoral relations committee. This will tend to reduce the chances of a destructive or immobilizing conflict between the pastor and the congregation. In general, every pastor should view that group of new members as (a) persons with spiritual and personal needs that must be identified, surfaced, and met, (b) creative allies in combatting passivity, and (c) potential members of a support group for the minister.

In summary, new members are different! When those differences can be perceived as a creative and productive resource, rather than as a threat or liability, your new members can be a very significant factor in responding to passivity, in developing and implementing a church growth strategy, and in preparing for a new era in your congregation's future!

CHAPTER SIX

PASSIVITY DURING
THE HONEYMOON

That first year of a new pastorate can be described in many different ways. One of the most widely used analogies is to refer to it as the honeymoon. This is the period during which the newly arrived minister and the congregation become better acquainted. Each discovers the unique personality of the other. Each identifies both strengths and flaws in the other that were not visible during the courtship. Each is forming opinions about the other, and these opinions will influence many different decisions during the years to come.

In the small membership congregation the people will seek to discover whether the new minister really loves them, or whether this is merely a post-seminary apprenticeship or a stepping-stone in the new minister's career. In the large congregations the leaders will seek to discover whether the new minister is an aggressive leader who is willing to take the initiative or is a reactive leader who waits and responds to the initiative of others and to changing circumstances.

Another perspective on that honeymoon of a new pastorate is to look at the congregation in terms of the theme of this book. Is the new minister greeted by an active congregation that is looking to the new pastor to help them on a journey that is already underway? Or will the new pastor encounter a group of people who are passively waiting for the new leader to point out the direction and announce, "Follow me! This is the way the Lord is calling us to go!"

One response to that distinction, to go back to the use of size in classifying congregations, is that the smaller congregations usually are hoping the new minister will be a person-centered, relational, loving, and affirming pastor who will be their shepherd. By contrast, most of the leaders, *but not all the members*, in the larger churches will be hoping that the new minister will be a combination of an inspiring preacher, a leader with a challenging vision of what the Lord has in mind for that parish, and a sheep dog who will snap at the heels of the slower-moving members.

If the frame of reference is changed from looking at congregations by size to looking at the statistical probability of what the new minister will encounter, a different picture emerges. At least one-third (and it may be closer to one-half) of all newly arrived pastors encounter in those first weeks what can be described as a passive congregation. Several of the more common sources of that passivity were described earlier in the second chapter. One strategy, which is the theme of the second, third, and fourth chapters, is to identify the source(s) of passivity and tailor a response accordingly.

Another perspective, widely shared among the laity, is that the pastor is the key to a productive response to passivity in the church. For those holding this point of view, including many ministers and denominational leaders, that first year of a new pastorate is the critical period in combatting passivity in a congregation.

How can a minister who has just moved to a new pastorate get the most mileage out of that first year? What can he or she do during those first months that will strengthen the foundations for ministry in the years to follow? What should be the major emphasis during those first several months? What is the best response of the new pastor to what appears to be a passive church?

One piece of conventional wisdom suggests a comparatively passive and nondirective role during that first year. "Get acquainted with the people." "Build the trust level." "Visit in every home." "Don't rock the boat." "Study the situation and discover the priorities." These are some of the more frequently heard admonitions to the minister who is moving to a new pastorate.

After studying scores of congregations that have recently completed their first year or two with a new minister, and after listening to thousands of lay persons from these same churches describe their reactions to that honeymoon year, the evidence strongly suggests that in the majority of cases the newly arrived minister should accept a more active leadership role.

Caution!

Most of the suggestions that follow should prove to be useful to a large proportion of the ministers who are about to move into a new (that is, new to that minister) pastorate. There are, however, certain types of situations that require a different approach by the newly arrived pastor. This can be illustrated by offering four examples where a different strategy would be appropriate.

Perhaps the most common exception is the severely divided congregation. This division might reflect sharp differences in an understanding of the nature, role, and purpose of the worshiping congregation, a conflict surrounding the departure of the new minister's immediate predecessor, a family feud, or some other issue in the decision-making process. In these situations the newly arrived pastor might be well advised to heed the conventional wisdom mentioned earlier and concentrate on a healing ministry. Occasionally this will also include rebuilding a positive image of the minister as a person and as a professional.

Another example is the minister who arrives immediately

following the termination of a long pastorate of fifteen years or longer, or who follows a pastor who died under tragic circumstances, such as an automobile accident, a suicide, or a sudden fatal illness. In perhaps three out of four of these situations, the newly arrived minister might do well to conceptualize this as an intentionally interim and relatively brief transitional pastorate and concentrate on laying the foundation for an effective pastorate by the next minister.

If *both* the new pastor and the lay leadership are able to impersonally analyze the dynamics of the situation, it may be possible for the new minister both to serve as the "intentional interim" and to "succeed" himself or herself by planning a new chapter to follow that two- three- four-year transitional chapter. This can happen. It has happened. It usually requires, however, a minister who is both personally and professionally a very secure person, and several perceptive lay leaders with a high level of competence in conceptualizing abstract ideas.

A third exception is the minister who comes to serve a congregation where a substantial portion of the members have walked out over some internal congregational or doctrinal dispute. They may or may not have been led in this departure by the former pastor, and they may or may not have gone out to organize a new congregation. Those details are not as significant as the hurt that was left behind when a portion of the congregation departed under less than friendly circumstances. In this situation the most creative lay leadership probably will come largely from those members who joined after the division and who have no firsthand recollection of the pain and grief that resulted from the split. Therefore the newly arrived pastor in this situation probably should concentrate her or his efforts on bringing new people into membership in that congregation and encouraging the election of some of the new members to leadership positions (see chapter 5 for several reasons why new members should be seen as assets).

The fourth exception is the parish in which the respect of the members for the office of pastor has been severely undermined by the actions of the predecessor. Unfortunately, this happens more frequently than people like to believe. When the newly arrived pastor encounters this situation, a high priority must be given to rebuilding the trust and respect the people have for that office.

Five Important Assumptions

In the vast majority of situations, however, in which the newly arrived minister detects the signs of passivity in the congregation, it may be more helpful for him or her to think in terms of developing a strategy or plan for that honeymoon year. While it is obvious that each such plan must be tailored to the sources of the passivity in that specific situation and the gifts of that particular minister, it may be helpful to suggest several items that could be included in this formulation of a strategy by the new minister.

This whole concept is based on five significant assumptions. First, one word that partially explains the concept of discipleship is *intentionality*. The call to ministry is a call to intentionality.

Second, the minister is a leader, and leaders lead. Leaders accept the responsibility for taking the initiative in a situation. The pastor is the *professional* leader in the church. This concept of a pro-active leadership style by the pastor is assumed to have special relevance to (a) the newly arrived pastor who is faced by a passive congregation, regardless of size, (b) the pastor of nearly all large congregations, and (c) the pastor in those denominations, such as Lutheran, Reformed Church in America, Episcopal, Christian Reformed Church, Presbyterian, Seventh-day Adventist, and Roman Catholic, in which the office of minister is held in unusually high esteem by the laity.

Third, those first several months often have tremendous

135

influence on the subsequent expectations that congregation of people have of their new minister. During that first year the new minister "trains" the people in what they can or cannot expect of their pastor during subsequent years. The minister who radically changes her leadership style or his priorities after that first year should assume that he or she will have to "retrain" the members to a new set of expectations.

Fourth—and the central thesis of this chapter—in a large proportion of congregations, the newly arrived minister encounters a passive congregation that says, "You lead us. Tell us what your goals are, Pastor, and we'll do what you want. We assume you brought your program with you. Go ahead and implement it." Unless the minister breaks this pattern of passivity within the first several months, he will place himself in a very vulnerable position.

Fifth, this concept of an intentional strategy for that first year assumes that the minister's responsibility is primarily to "cause things to happen" rather than to "do it" unilaterally. This last assumption, which distinguishes between a leadership style of the pastor "doing it" and an approach that produces a widespread and very active lay involvement in "causing things to happen," is of central importance in breaking that cycle of passivity.

This is not the same as the popular understanding of the more passive "enabler" role for the pastor.[1] This last assumption requires a very active and initiating role for the newly arrived minister! It is often more difficult to cause things to happen than to do them by oneself. Among other things, this means changing that naturally passive stance of the laity.

A Strategy Checklist

After reflecting on these cautions and assumptions, the newly arrived pastor may be prepared to begin to develop a strategy for that first year. One way of doing this is to build a checklist as the basis for that strategy. Here are a few suggestions for that checklist.

1. Do Not Try to Outpassive the Passive!

The temptation awaiting the new minister in the passive church is to wait for the laity to take the initiative. "I'll wait for them to tell me what they want to do here. After all, I'm called to be a preacher and a servant, not a general."

This passive stance by the new minister probably will produce one or more of four responses from the congregation. These are (a) continued passivity, (b) an over-adaptation, or apparent support for whatever the new minister proposes, but few active allies who will invest the time, energy, and creativity to implement the new pastor's proposals, (c) agitation and discontent over the new minister's "lack of initiative" and "inability to lead," and/or (d) some type of internal disruption—and this may result in the premature departure of the minister.

A better response by the new minister to what appears to be a passive church is to build a strategy that includes *at least* the next three points from this checklist.

2. Plan from Strength

Every congregation has its own strengths and weaknesses. The newly arrived minister will be subjected to considerable pressure to concentrate on these weaknesses of the church in its program and outreach. If that weakness or need corresponds to a strength or gift of the new minister, it may be tempting for the pastor to build a strategy on responding to that weakness. Frequently he or she "succeeds" with this strategy. Common examples of this include the gifted preacher who produces a 50 percent increase in worship attendance during that first year, the bright young man who doubles the size of the youth group within several months, or the magnetic personality who specializes in calling on the unchurched people in the community and adds dozens of names to the membership roll in a remarkably short period of time. The results of this strategy usually include (a) the admiration and favorable comments of the church members, especially those who blamed the preceding minister for whatever the weaknesses or shortcomings of the congregation may be, (b) a reinforcement of the passive stance of the congregation—if the energetic new minister will do all the work, the laity will encourage that and feed her efforts with flattery, (c) a gradual aging of the congregation's leadership as new people are received into membership, but not accepted into the fellowship of the congregation, (d) a tired minister who each year has to exceed the performance of the previous year, (e) a sharp decline in participation and activity when that minister eventually departs after what may turn out to be a relatively brief pastorate, *or* a long-term and very productive pastorate that comes to an end with the burned-out pastor leaving the professional ministry, (f) a strengthening of the conviction held by many lay persons that getting the right minister is the secret to building a strong church, and (g) placing a heavy burden on the next minister who will be expected to top that act.

A better strategy is to seek to identify two areas of strength that are complementary and mutually reinforcing. One is the special talents or gifts of the newly arrived minister. What do you as a minister do best?

The second is the major strength or assets of the congregation. A representative example of this is the minister who came to the congregation that recently had completed the twelve-year process of relocating and building a new meeting place. When this effort was completed, the congregation was distressed to discover they had more building than program and that people were not standing in line to join this congregation to help pay off the mortgage on their beautiful new meeting place.

One of the hidden price tags on the relocation effort had been the diversion of the time and energy of the laity from ministry and program to real estate and finances. While some other ministers saw the new building and the large debt as liabilities, the newly arrived pastor identified his own strengths in retraining and developing lay leadership, initiating new program and teacher-training experiences as complementing the asset of a building designed primarily for a strong teaching ministry. In three years the Christian education program had tripled in size and also served as the primary evangelistic thrust of this congregation, as well as producing new opportunities for the active personal and spiritual growth of the members.

The best strategy for the new minister facing a passive congregation is to identify, affirm, and build on the complementary strengths of both the pastor and the congregation!

3. Look for an Early Victory!

Several decades ago one congregation borrowed $14,000 from the denomination at 3 percent annual interest to complete a building program. The understanding at the time that this debt was incurred was that the congregation would not be expected to repay this loan until after it had retired all its other indebtedness. Twenty-two years later, and six years after the last payment on the last of the remaining mortgages had been made, this congregation was paying $420 in interest annualy on this $14,000 debt. "Why should we pay off a debt at 3 percent interest when we can receive 8 to 9 percent on any money we accumulate in our savings account?" was the response of the finance committee chairman whenever anyone suggested this debt should be repaid.

A new minister arrived in May. In September he took the initiative and suggested from the pulpit that if each of the 220 families would contribute an average of $10 a month for four months, this could be combined with a $6,000 unrestricted bequest the congregation had recently received and that debt could be retired as a Christmas present from the congregation to the denomination. This proposal was enthusiastically endorsed by the members, many of whom felt that the congregation had failed to meet a moral obligation. The entire $14,000 was raised from designated giving, leaving the bequest untouched. Even the chairman of the finance committee was pleased, since this did not require using any of the accumulated surplus which he guarded so carefully. The passive stance of the congregation was changed to an active role, a moral obligation was met, a sense of progress surfaced, and the congregation celebrated a victory with the new minister.

Another way of describing the same approach is for the newly arrived pastor to encourage completion of an unfinished task. Examples of this include bringing a group of people together to compile a complete and accurate membership roster, encouraging the trustees to incorporate the congregation if that has not been done, assembling a work crew to clean the church and yard if that is necessary, scheduling one or two major festival events such as a Christmas Eve worship service, a Reformation Sunday service, or a series of Lenten services if this had not been the practice, planning an annual leadership training event for all newly elected church leaders, or celebrating the founding of the congregation with a major event every year.

These are all simple, nonthreatening, and easy to understand action proposals that will not overwhelm anyone with their complexity, and each provides for an active role for the laity.

4. Set Short-Term Goals

A common cliché suggests, "Any group without achievable and measurable goals flounders!" This deserves the serious attention of the newly arrived pastor who is responding to a passive congregation. This new minister is in an excellent position to help the congregation, as it sees itself writing a new chapter in its history, to set some specific, attainable, measurable, and visible goals that can be achieved within two or three years.

A useful way of initiating this is to ask, in that first round of parish visitation, "Every person has some wish for the church. What is your favorite wish for this church? What would you like to see us accomplish here together during the next year or two? Please make your wish as specific as possible and suggest something that is realistically possible for us to accomplish in a year or so."

This will bring a few responses on the same visit during which the wish is solicited. Others will come a few days or a few weeks later as people have had time to reflect on this request. A useful procedure, about six months after the seeds have been planted in the first parish visits by the newly arrived minister, is to pass out blank 4 x 6 cards during the worship service and ask people to write their wishes on these cards. A planning committee can take these cards and use them in setting short-term goals for the church. It helps if there is a clear stipulation that no one will sign their "I wish" card *unless they are willing to help turn that wish into reality.*

This again is a means of changing the naturally passive stance of the members to a more active role and also of building goals on the desires and needs of the people, rather than on the new minister's program.

Usually these short-term goals take the form of unfinished tasks that should have been completed earlier. This often means that the far more complex undertaking of redefining role (see chapter 3), which often must be completed before formulating major long-term goals, can be postponed until the second or third year of that pastorate. In general, it is more productive when this redefinition of role is undertaken from an active, rather than a passive stance.

Sir Isaac Newton's first law of motion is that a body in motion tends to remain in motion, and a body at rest tends to remain at rest. This property of matter, called *inertia*, is also found in institutions. The new pastor of a congregation "at rest" may decide it is advisable to get that body in motion and utilize the power of Newton's first law, before tackling the more complex and difficult task of redefining role.

5. Call on the Exploited

Nearly every congregation has a subtle, but very significant distinction between the workers and the leaders. The leaders set policy, secure recognition for their leadership contributions, and usually are held in high esteem by themselves and by the rest of the members. The workers, such as the Sunday school teachers, the callers, the ladies in the kitchen, and those who run the errands, tend to be neglected. They rarely receive the recognition, the thank-you's, and the visibility granted the leaders. The new pastor can learn much, and accomplish even more, by systematicaly calling on the workers of the church with only one agenda item. That item is the question, "How does it go with you? Tell me how things are going with you." Sympathetic calls on the workers of the congregation in which the newly arrived pastor has the role of an active listener can be a very productive investment of time during those first several months. The larger the congregation, the more important is this element of a total strategy.

As was pointed out in the previous chapter, some of the workers, and especially new members, may be very productive allies in developing a creative response to passivity.

6. Call on the Angry, the Alienated, and the Inactive

The conventional wisdom suggests the newly arrived minister should give priority in calling to the leaders and pillars of the church. Some of the most productive calling, however, during the first few months, will be the calls made on the angry, the alienated, and the inactive members. Again, the new minister often will assume the role of the "active listener." Frequently this requires two or three visits to the same home. At first the new minister hears the polite excuses. Subsequently the real reasons for the hurt begin to surface. Only after these have been uncovered, after the first few layers of excuses have been peeled away, will it be possible for anyone to do anything about that hurt. To be most effective, this calling must be done within the first two or three months following the arrival of the new minister.

There are very important values that can be achieved through this series of calls. First, and most important, members who feel neglected, ignored, overlooked, and alienated receive some attention.

Second, about seven-eighths of the hurts and pains can be cured by the active listening stance of the newly arrived minister. The other 10 to 15 percent are beyond the scope of this treatment, however, and the new pastor should not expect to bat a thousand in these calls.

Third, some, but not all, of the inactive and alienated members will move over to an active role as a result of this series of visits.

Fourth, a few of these inactive members may become very productive allies in program development and in changing a passive congregation into an active one.

Finally, there is Sir Isaac Newton's law of motion. For every action there is an equal and opposite reaction. This law also applies to the formerly passive parish that has become an active congregation with the help of the new pastor. One way to minimize the negative impact of that reaction is for the new pastor to call on and listen to those who have been overlooked and are now angry and alienated, also the pillars of the past (represented by Martha White in the previous chapter), as well as on potential allies.

7. Legitimatize the Grief

In nearly every congregation some of the members feel a sense of loss and grief over the departure of the previous pastor and/or that minister's family. In many cases this grief becomes a major barrier to the effective ministry of the new pastor. This is especially true when the new minister arrives within days, or even within a few weeks, of the departure of the predecessor. The new minister should openly legitimatize that grief, encourage people to talk about it, recognize it as a normal human reaction, and not feel threatened by it.

By affirming the members' grief as natural and normal, the new minister strengthens the pastoral relationship with the people faster.

In general, grief moves people to a passive stance, and the new minister should recognize that responding to the grief over the departure of the predecessor may be the first, and one of the most essential, steps in breaking that cycle of passivity.

8. Build a New Leadership Team

The ideal leadership team in a parish includes lay persons who complement the minister's gifts, skills, and talents. This is a widely accepted concept.

What complicates the picture, however, are three other factors. First, a change of pastors frequently produces a radical change in the gifts, skills, and talents possessed by the minister. This is especially true in the call system churches where there is a pronounced tendency, when seeking a new minister, to give top priority to finding a pastor who is strong in the areas where the predecessor was perceived to be weak.

Second, a minister frequently moves when a congregation is ready for a change in its agenda. This may be following the completion of a building program, when the agenda should be changed to ministry and program. It may be a change in the role of a congregation from decades as a family-oriented church to a new role as an adult-oriented congregation. It may be a change from a member-oriented focus to an outreach focus, or vice versa. This change may require a new leadership team.

Third, as was pointed out in chapter 4, sometimes the leadership team has developed a very high level of competence in permission-withholding, but has very little practice or skill in permission-giving.

This often means that the newly arrived minister finds a leadership group chosen to complement the gifts and talents of the predecessor, but who are uncomfortable with a new agenda, with a pro-active pastor, or with any efforts to disturb that comfortable complacency that is a part of a permission-withholding stance.

In the smaller church this often will require a major effort in retraining the lay leaders for a new role and a new agenda. In large congregations this may mean replacing a large proportion of the lay leaders with new leaders who naturally are more comfortable with the new set of relationships and the new agenda. In the middle-sized congregation this probably means retraining some of the members of the leadership team and replacing others.

The new pastor who assumes that the old leadership team will automatically be appropriate for the new era may be creating problems with that assumption.

9. Plan to Stay

There is overwhelmingly persuasive evidence that, from the congregation's long-term perspective, the best years of a pastorate rarely begin before the third, fourth, or fifth year of a pastorate. That is when the influence of the "new pastor" begins to have a positive long-term impact on that congregation. Those best years are more likely to begin with the seventh or eighth year rather than the first or second. Therefore a very important part of the strategy for the newly arrived minister may be to see this as potentially an eight- to twelve-year pastorate, rather than as a two- to four-year chapter in a career filled with many, many different pastorates.

10. Celebrate Every Victory!

One of the most effective methods for reducing passivity and for reinforcing the sense of momentum in a congregation is to lift up and celebrate every victory. These include that early victory mentioned previously in this checklist, the implementation of the short-term goals, the celebration of the annual anniversary of the founding of that parish, the organization of every new face-to-face group or class, the acceptance of a new challenge in outreach, the completion of a successful financial campaign, the reception of a class of new members, the development of a new community ministry, the remodeling or refurbishing of the meeting place, the creation of a new choir or musical group, the recovery of a member from a serious illness or injury, the birth of every new baby, the completion of a special project by the youth group, the anniversary of the adult Sunday school class, the final payment on the mortgage, the inauguration of a new program on radio or cable TV, the organization of a new church school class for one group of handicapped persons, the successful completion of the vacation Bible school, that special achievement of the women's organization, or the addition of a new staff member.

Every victory should be lifted up and celebrated, and thanks given to God for his blessings.

Now, if you are a newly arrived pastor, how many of these ten points can you fit into your strategy for that new pastorate?

CHAPTER SEVEN

WHAT ARE YOUR ASSUMPTIONS?

"I often wonder how that new independent Baptist church out on the west side of town is able to get its people so involved," reflected Myrtle Phillips to two close friends. These three long-time members of Highland Church were eating lunch together on a beautiful September day. "Their parking lot is filled with cars on Sunday morning, every Sunday evening and on Wednesday nights, as well as on one or two other nights during the week. Whenever I drive by there, I see something going on. How do they get their people to be so active?

"I've often wondered about that myself," replied one of her friends. "Many of our members are very busy, and we have so many in nursing homes or shut-ins, that we could never get the turnout they do. I've been a member here at Highland Church for over fifty years now, and it's not like it used to be. Years ago we had Sunday evening services, and we had prayer meeting every Wednesday night, but I know you couldn't get people out to either one today. Between the competition of television, camping and the shopping malls, on the one hand, and so many working wives, on the other, I sometimes think we do pretty well to get as many out on Sunday morning as we do."

147

"I guess you're right," agreed Myrtle. "The kids grow up and move away, and so many of us have carried the load for so long that we're all getting tired, I guess."

"I'll tell you what the difference is between that congregation you're talking about and Highland Church," offered the third member of this luncheon group. "That church demands a lot more of its members than we do. That preacher warns the people that if they don't shape up and do what they're supposed to do, they'll end up in hell. Sometimes I think our minister ought to put more emphasis on making our people live up to their membership vows. I think he's too easygoing and afraid he might upset some of the big contributors."

This conversation illustrates several of the basic assumptions that will influence the content of any congregation's strategy for mission, for motivating members, and for combatting the natural institutional drift toward passivity. There may be value in bringing up a half-dozen questions that will help expose some of these assumptions.

The first of these concerns two basic principles of human association. Do you assume that your congregation is "glued together" by a *shared commitment* to a common interest? Or do you assume that the dominant principle holding your congregation together is a *legal* structure?[1]

While it is impossible to find any congregation organized solely around one of these two principles, these two organizing principles for voluntary associations do offer a frame of reference that can be useful in understanding what is happening and why.

If one thinks in terms of a spectrum, the concept of a voluntary association organized around the shared commitments of the members would be at one end of this spectrum. A bridge club, an amateur softball team, the Southern Baptist Convention, the group that gathers for dinner on the third Saturday of every month, the local ministerial association, or the typical adult Sunday school class would be examples of this type of voluntary association.

At the other end of the spectrum would be the voluntary association created around a series of formal rules with clearly defined and articulated expectations of each member, perhaps even including annual dues or a membership fee. The county bar association, the National Football League, the American Medical Association, and the United Presbyterian Church in the United States of America are examples of voluntary associations located closer to that end of the spectrum emphasizing the legal principle for organizing a voluntary association.

Most Protestant congregations are located somewhere along the broad middle of this spectrum. By contrast, the denominations are scattered all along the entire spectrum. The United Presbyterian Church in the U. S. A., for example, is located near the end marked "legal principle," while the Christian Church (Disciples of Christ), the United Church of Christ, and the Unitarian Universalist Association are at the other end of this spectrum, labeled "shared commitment." A dozen other denominations, including The United Methodist Church, the Episcopal Church, the Presbyterian Church in the U. S. A., and the American Lutheran Church are scattered along the spectrum between those two extreme points.

From that brief conversation at the beginning of this chapter it appears that a legal structure, with its formally and clearly stated rules of obligations and responsibilities, is the primary organizing principle in that new independent Baptist church.

Without even looking at its denominational label, it appears that the long-established Highland Church is located near the other end of that spectrum, labeled "shared commitment."

Now, why bring that up here?

There are four reasons why this is a useful frame of reference for looking at churches. First, the appropriate behavior for a leader in a church with a strong emphasis on a legal principle of association may be counterproductive behavior for a leader in a church built on the principle of share commitments. In other words, what may be appropriate and productive behavior for the minister of that independent Baptist church may not be appropriate behavior at Highland Church. One of the differences, as was pointed out in chapters 1 and 5, is that in most new congregations, and among many new members in all churches, there is a strong emphasis on the religious needs of the people and on that vertical commitment to God. By contrast, in the long-established congregation, one of the most important dynamics of congregational life is the horizontal commitment of the members to one another. That may be one of the reasons why that new Baptist congregation has a higher level of member participation than the long-established Highland Church, which includes many people who have been members for two or three decades or longer.

A second reason for lifting up this frame of reference is that voluntary associations built on shared commitments tend to be in competition with other voluntary associations based on the shared commitments of the members, for that limited supply of time and energy of the members. The voluntary association built around a legal principle is less vulnerable to this competition.

When this second point is translated into local church terms, a complex generalization emerges. Congregations like this independent Baptist church tend to attract as members persons who are not likely to be heavily involved in those voluntary associations based on shared commitments. Thus the congregation located toward the legal end of this spectrum tends to draw persons into its membership who are not faced with a conflict in loyalties. The loyalty to their church, which emphasizes that legal principle, comes first.

Their allegiance to some other voluntary association that is built around the principle of shared commitment, comes second.

By contrast, the congregation, such as Highland Church, that places a greater emphasis on the relational dimensions of organizational life, and that is organized around the principle of shared commitment, tends to attract as members those persons who often are involved in other voluntary associations also created around that principle of shared commitment. These members repeatedly are faced with competing pressures for their time and energy from these other voluntary associations. These competing demands are more difficult for the members to resolve. This helps to explain why some churches have been hostile to lodges and other private societies. It also helps explain why that independent Baptist church feels less competition for the members' time than is felt at Highland Church.

Third, every voluntary association, regardless of whether it was created primarily on the legal principle of association or primarily on the basis of a shared commitment of the members, tends to move in the direction of being dominated by the legal principle. This generalization helps to explain the increase in the quantity of litigation in the long-established Protestant denominations. It also helps to explain why the air is filled with so many "oughts" in long-established congregations, but most of those "oughts" are ignored by those who believe it is a voluntary association based on a shared commitment. This also helps to explain why the third member of that luncheon trio wanted a more legalistic stance to be taken by their minister.

Finally, this drift in the direction of a legal basis for association may be interrupted, and at least temporarily severed, when that voluntary association is confronted with an extreme emergency or a crisis. This generalization helps explain why the passive congregation, in which the increasing number of legalistic admonitions had had little effect, suddenly became an active, closely knit, and caring fellowship the day after the fire completely destroyed the eighty-five-year-old meeting place of the congregation.

Now, what is your assumption about where your congregation is located on that spectrum? Do other leaders agree with your assumptions? How does that inform your strategy for planning for ministry? What does it say about combatting passivity?

A second basic assumption illustrated by the conversation at the beginning of this chapter concerns the role of the minister. Do you assume the pastor is the key to combatting passivity in a church? Or do you assume the laity should and will take the initiative? Does the size of the congregation influence your assumption? Does the length of tenure of the members and of the minister speak to that assumption?[2]

The third assumption to be raised here goes back to chapter 5. Do you assume those new members are carbon copies of the long-time members? Or do you assume the new members possess some unique characteristics that merit consideration? Does that help explain some of the differences between that new Baptist church, where everyone is a new member, and the Highland Church with many long-time members?

A fourth assumption that was illustrated by the earlier conversation concerns the age of the congregation. Would you expect the long-established Highland Church to resemble that new independent Baptist church? Or would you assume the two to be quite different from each other, simply because of how long each has been in existence?

How does that assumption speak to a strategy for planning for ministry? How does that assumption speak to your congregation? How long ago was it established?

While it did not come through clearly in that conversation, a fifth assumption did surface. How do you see the call to renewal in the church? Do you assume renewal means a restoration of old values, a rejuvenation of old programs, and a return to the old schedule? Or does it mean new wineskins for the new wine of a new day to serve a new generation? How widespread is the agreement—or disagreement—on that assumption in your congregation?

Or, to go back to the opening illustration, should the leaders at Highland Church seek to copy that new independent Baptist church in order to achieve a parallel level of member participation? Or should the leaders at Highland Church assume that God has a distinct and different role in mind for them?

Finally, the last of these six assumptions was illustrated by Myrtle Phillips as she responded to her second friend's analysis of the differences between that new independent Baptist congregation and Highland Church where she has been a faithful member for so many years.

"I agree with you that high expectations do make a difference," replied Myrtle. "My husband used to say that the way to make people great is to ask a lot of them. When people are challenged to respond beyond what they believe to be their capability, that makes them grow. Maybe that's what that minister is doing over at that Baptist church, but I don't know. What I do know is that God has a place in his world for Highland Church and part of our job is to discover what he has in mind for us. I really don't believe we should try to copy what some other church is doing. I think what we should do is open the doors to let the Holy Spirit in to guide and direct us. I believe we can open doors to the Holy Spirit or we can close them. Maybe we've closed a few doors that need to be opened. Maybe that's the best approach to overcoming the lethargy and complacency among some of our people at Highland."

What is your response to these comments? What is the assumption about the power and direction of the Holy Spirit that guides the planning and decision-making processes in your church? Do you believe your congregation can either open or close doors to the Holy Spirit? What do you understand that God has in mind as the role for the congregation of which you are a member?

NOTES

INTRODUCTION

1. For an excellent review essay of the research on the impact of the changes of the past three decades, and their implications for the generation born after World War II, see Douglas Alan Walrath, "Why Some People May Go Back to Church," *Review of Religious Research*, vol. 21, no. 4 (Supplement 1980) pp. 468-75.

Chapter One

1. David McCullough, *The Path Between the Seas* (New York: Simon & Schuster, 1977), p. 141.

2. A useful application of this approach for helping urban churches define their role is William Baird, *The Corinthian Church—A Biblical Approach to Urban Culture* (Nashville: Abingdon Press, 1964).

3. For a provocative and corrective review of the definition of the word "community," see Thomas Bender, *Community and Social Change in America* (New Brunswick, N.J.: Rutgers University Press, 1978).

4. A brief description of the characteristics of churches in different size categories can be found in Lyle E. Schaller, *The Multiple Staff and the Larger Church* (Nashville: Abingdon, 1980), pp. 15-50. For an excellent introduction to the internal dynamics of the small church, see Carl S. Dudley, *Making the Small Church Effective* (Nashville: Abingdon, 1978), pp. 19-45.

5. H. Paul Douglass and Edmund De S. Brunner, *The Protestant Church as a Social Institution* (New York: Harper & Bros., 1935), p. 87.

6. Laurence M. Hepple, *The Church in Rural Missouri, Part V: Rural-Urban Churches Compared*, Research Bulletin 633E (Columbia, Missouri Agricultural Experiment Station, July 1959), p. 296.

7. For an extended discussion of the place of music in the large church, see Lyle E. Schaller, "Music in the Large Church," *Choristers Guild Letters* (March 1980), pp. 123-25.

8. For a more detailed examination of the impact of polity, see Paul M. Harrison, *Authority and Power in the Free Church Tradition* (Carbondale, Ill.: Southern Illinois University Press, 1971); H. Richard Niebuhr, *The Social Sources of Denominationalism* (New Gloucester, Mass.: Peter Smith, 1963); Robert Lee, *The Social Sources of Church Unity* (Nashville: Abingdon Press, 1960); Lyle E. Schaller, *The Decision-Makers* (Nashville: Abingdon Press, 1974); Paul A. Mickey and Robert L. Wilson, *What New Creation?* (Nashville: Abingdon, 1977); Richard G. Hutcheson, Jr., *Wheel Within the Wheel* (Atlanta: John Knox Press, 1979); and *Report of the Task Force on Polity and Reconciliation* (New York: Office of the General Assembly, 1980).

9. Dean M. Kelley, *Why Conservative Churches Are Growing: A Study in Sociology of Religion* (San Francisco: Harper & Row, 1972). For his own reappraisal of his thesis, see Kelley's "Preface to the Paperback Edition" (1977), and "Why Conservative Churches Are Still Growing," *Journal for the Scientific Study of Religion*, vol. 17, (1978) pp. 165-72. For two incisive critiques of Kelley's thesis, see Reginald W. Bibby, "Why Conservative Churches *Really* Are Growing: Kelley Revisited," *Journal for the Scientific Study of Religion*, vol. 17, (1978) 129-37; and Carl S. Dudley, *Where Have All Our People Gone?* (New York: Pilgrim Press, 1979), pp. 47-52. For a discussion of the implications of different types of commitment, see Lyle E. Schaller, *Hey That's Our Church!* (Nashville: Abingdon Press, 1975) pp. 34-38.

10. James David Barber, *The Presidential Character* (Englewood Cliffs, N.J.: Prentice-Hall, 1977).

11. Roger G. Barker, *Ecological Psychology* (Stanford Univer-

sity Press, 1968), pp. 18-34. For an interpretation of Barker's work and its application to church planning, see Lyle E. Schaller, *Effective Church Planning* (Nashville: Abingdon, 1979), pp. 26-55 and 68-92.

12. Carl S. Dudley, "Neighborhood Churches in Changing Communities," *New Conversations* (Spring 1978), p. 9.

13. Walter Brueggemann, *The Prophetic Imagination* (Philadelphia: Fortress Press, 1978), p. 13.

14. This concept of "pushing the product" comes from a very creative book on combatting institutional blight in an organization, Theodore Levitt, *Innovation in Marketing* (New York: McGraw-Hill Book Co., 1962).

Chapter Two

1. Pierre Mornell, *Passive Men, Wild Women* (New York: Simon & Schuster, 1979).

2. For a more detailed description of the "landlord role" and the characteristics of this type of congregation, see Lyle E. Schaller and Charles A. Tidwell, *Creative Church Administration* (Nashville: Abingdon Press, 1975), pp. 183-91.

3. This concept is elaborated on in William Glasser, *The Identity Society* (New York: Harper & Row, 1972).

4. Henry J. Heimlich, *Home Guide to Emergency Medical Situations* (New York: Simon & Schuster, 1980), p. 15.

5. *Ibid.*, p. 16.

Chapter Three

1. Glasser, *The Identity Society*.

2. For an extensive analysis of this type of congregation in search of a new role, see Ezra Earl Jones and Robert L. Wilson, *What's Ahead for Old First Church?* (New York: Harper & Row, 1974).

3. For an introduction to the concept of the *intentional* interim minister, see Lyle E. Schaller, *Survival Tactics in the Parish* (Nashville: Abingdon, 1977), chap. 15.

4. Robert K. Greenleaf, *The Servant as Leader* (Cambridge: Massachusetts Center for Applied Studies, n.d.), p. 14.

Chapter Four

1. For a more detailed statement on the retraining of the lay leaders, see Lyle E. Schaller, *Survival Tactics in the Parish* (Nashville: Abingdon, 1977), pp. 104-10.

2. For an extended explanation of this concept of "counting the yes votes," see Schaller and Tidwell, *Creative Church Administration*, pp. 38-44.

Chapter Six

1. For a discussion of why the concept of the minister as enabler is the most difficult leadership style open to a pastor, see Lyle E. Schaller, "The Enabler: An Impossible Challenge" in *Effective Church Planning* (Nashville: Abingdon, 1979), pp. 166-70. While this leadership style has been advocated in many theological seminaries, very few teach the variety of skills necessary for a minister to be an effective enabler.

Chapter Seven

1. For this first point I am greatly indebted to the provocative insights in Lon L. Fuller, "Two Principles of Human Association" in *Voluntary Associations*, ed. J. Roland Pennock and John W. Chapman (New York: Atherton Press, 1969), pp. 3-23.

2. Two very useful books on the evolution of the role of the Protestant minister in America are Donald M. Scott, *From Office to Profession: The New England Ministry, 1750-1850* (Philadelphia: University of Pennsylvania Press, 1978); and William T. Youngs, Jr., *God Messengers: Religious Leadership in Colonial New England 1700-1750* (Baltimore: Johns Hopkins Press, 1976). For a very provocative review of Scott's book, emphasizing the minister's role as leader of a *voluntary* association, see Martin E. Marty, "Structure Without Comparison" in *American Journal of Sociology*, vol. 85, no. 1 (July 1979), pp. 178-82.

Two of the very best contemporary statements on an effective leadership style for the minister are to be found in Roger A. Johnson, *Congregations as Nurturing Communities: A Study of Nine Congregations of the Lutheran Church in America* (Philadelphia: Division for Parish Services, 1979), and Ernest T. Campbell, "They Also Serve Who Lead," *Pulpit Digest* (November-December 1979), pp. 7-10.